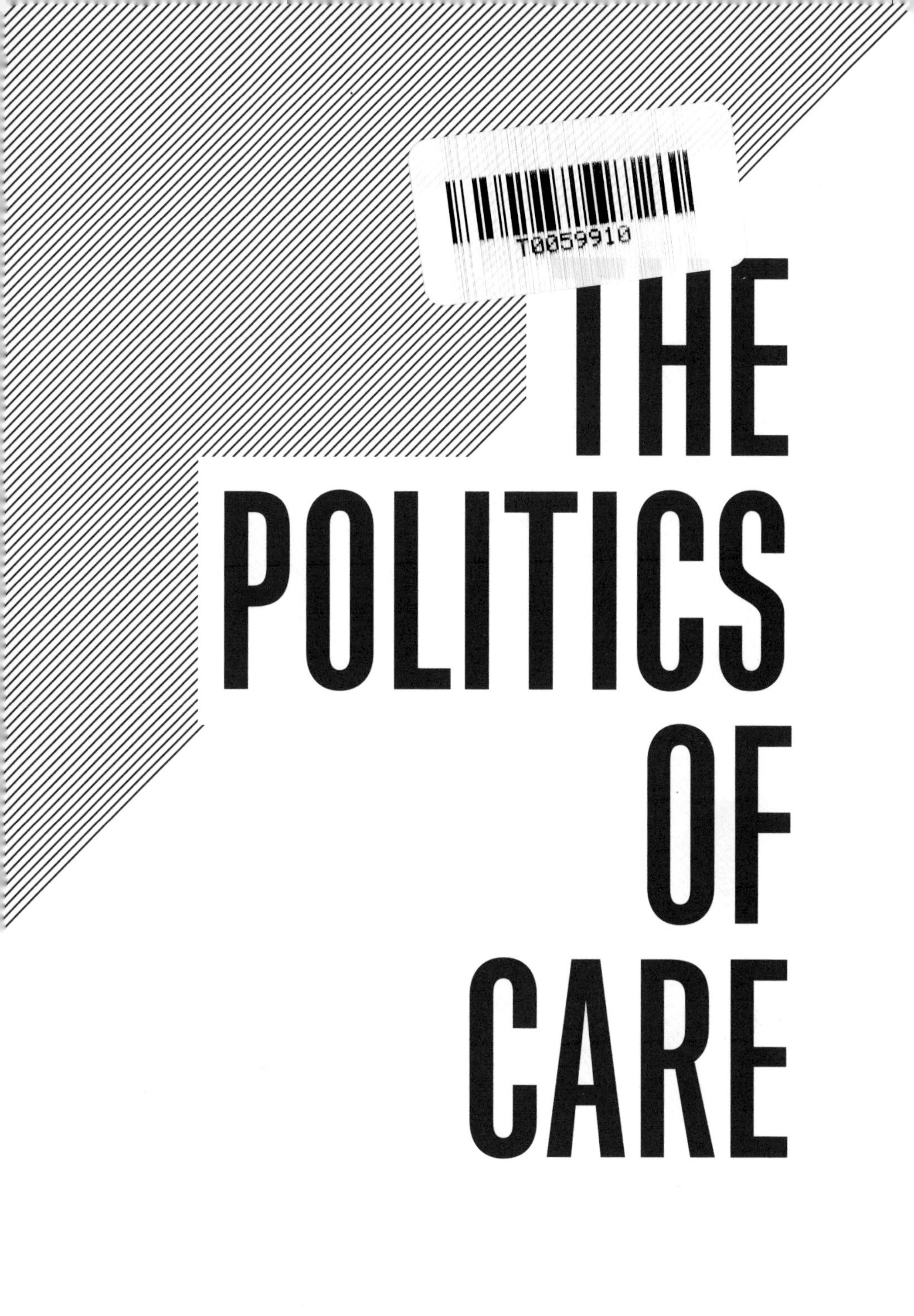
T0059910
THE
POLITICS
OF
CARE

THE POLITICS OF CARE

a copublication of
Boston Review & Verso Books

made possible by a generous grant from
The William and Flora Hewlett Foundation

The Politics of Care is *Boston Review* Forum 15 (45.3)

To become a member, visit
bostonreview.net/membership/

For questions about donations and major gifts,
contact Dan Manchon, dan@bostonreview.net

For questions about memberships, call 877-406-2443
or email Customer_Service@bostonreview.info.

Boston Review
PO Box 390568
Cambridge, MA 02139-0568

ISSN: 0734-2306 / ISBN: 978-1-83976-309-0

CONTENTS

COVID-19 AND POLITICAL CULTURES

NO ONE IS DISPOSABLE

EDITORS' NOTE

Deborah Chasman & Joshua Cohen

OVER THE PAST six months, the COVID-19 pandemic has upended our individual and social lives. As we write, it has killed at least 160,000 Americans and more than 700,000 people globally. Apocalyptic in the original meaning of the term—a disclosure or revelation—the pandemic has exposed the political and economic arrangements that enabled its terrible human devastation.

Working from home, feeling the sense of urgency, and hoping to respond constructively to the crisis, we nearly tripled our normal volume of *Boston Review* online publishing. Essays came from a mix of longtime contributors and new voices—thinkers who could speak directly to the moment, and who share our commitment to the power of collective reasoning and imagination to create a more just world. We called the series Thinking in a Pandemic.

And then we watched—with horror and indignation—the killing of George Floyd. So our efforts to provide a forum for people to speak to the pandemic—including the racial disparities in its impact—converged with our longstanding commitment to providing a forum for hard thinking about racial justice.

This volume includes some of the best of those separate but related efforts: clear-eyed looks at the pandemic and racism, along with ideas about the way toward a new kind of politics—what Gregg Gonsalves and Amy Kapczynski call "a politics of care"—that centers people's basic needs and connections to fellow citizens, the global community, and the natural world. The contributions draw on their authors' varied backgrounds—public health to philosophy, history to economics, literature to activism—but together they point to a future in which, as Simon Waxman writes, "no one is disposable."

—August 2020

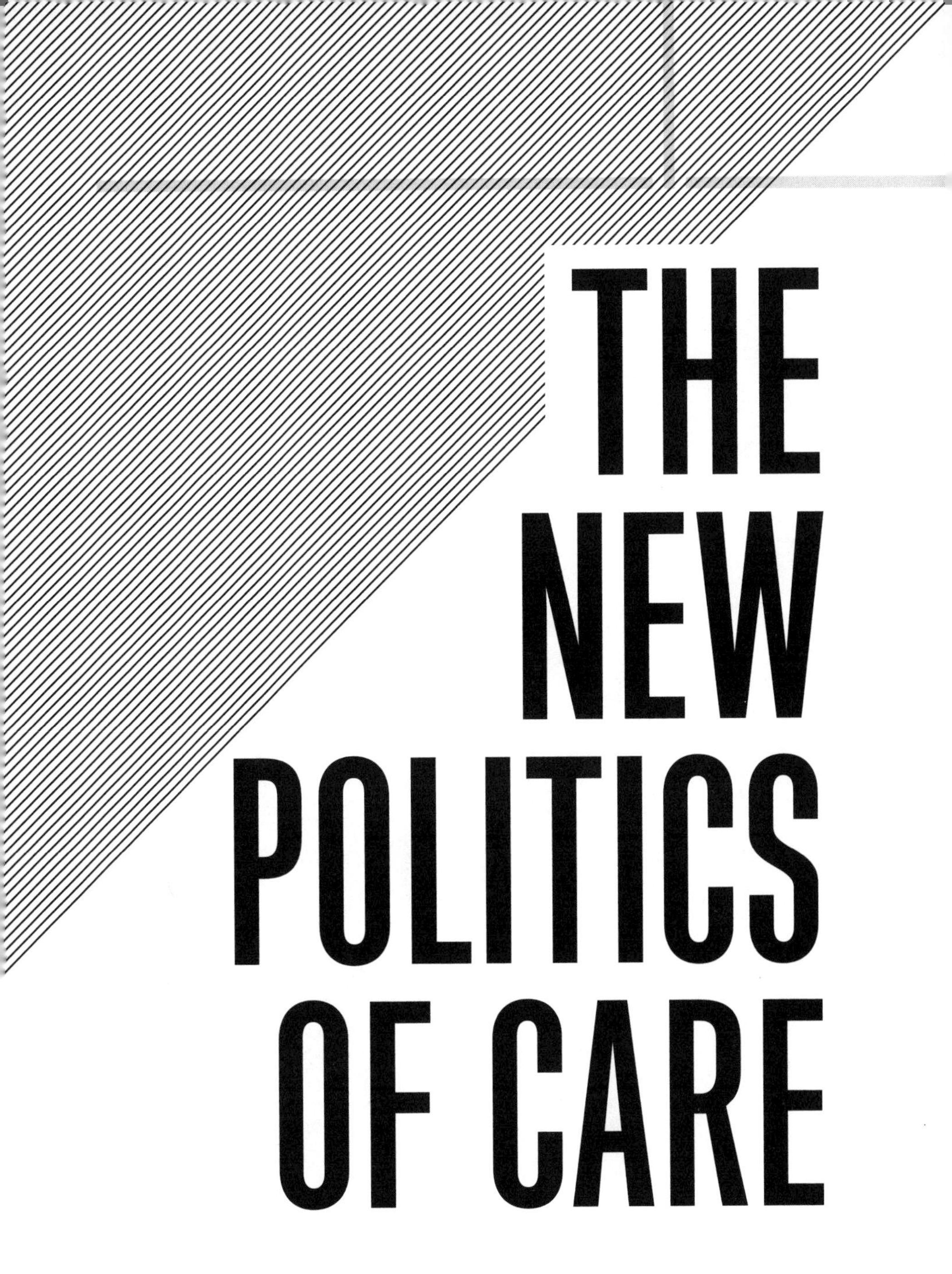

Gregg Gonsalves &
Amy Kapczynski

IN MARCH 2020 THE UNITED STATES surpassed China to become the country with the greatest number of confirmed COVID-19 cases in the world, and it has remained at the top of infection and mortality charts since. The scale of our failure is truly staggering. As of early August, more than 160,000 Americans have died from COVID-19—almost 25 percent of all deaths around the world in a country that accounts for just over 4 percent of the world's population. All the while, our façade of federal leadership has been ruinous. After more than six months of global emergency, President Donald Trump cannot think beyond the twenty-four-hour news cycle, now focused solely on his reelection campaign. Meanwhile, several states have rushed to reopen, even while new cases surge and a viable containment plan remains notional, at best—when the disease is not outright rejected as a hoax.

The first stage of the U.S. COVID-19 response was denial, issued straight from the top. The second was a wave of social solidarity as we realized that, in the absence of leadership, we had to act: communities, neighbors, and state and local governments began to try to flatten the curve. The third stage, the one we remain in, has been a riptide of skepticism—a powerful current running against the wave of social distancing, leading to an acceleration of the pandemic. An outbreak of armchair epidemiology and economics has aided and abetted the problem, suggesting we must choose between saving the vulnerable and "saving the economy." For Republicans this reframed choice obscures the fact that the Trump administration's catastrophic response systematically undermined our ability to shift to a more focused approach. At a minimum, that would have required massive testing and contact tracing, widespread distribution of personal protective equipment to the general public, structural supports to enable people to follow public health recommendations, and a scale up of our health care capacity.

That has not happened. Instead, we have seen millions of Americans sacrifice for one another in a remarkable display of care for their friends, families, and neighbors. It is telling, however, that our typical indicators of the economy register these actions as a kind of collective suicide. "The economy" that we're offered in the usual take—measuring little and commanding much—is a death machine, as climate activists have been saying for years. Models of the economy do not incorporate the idea of *staying home* as productive of anything—not least avoidance of the negative externality of mass death. Staying home, taking care of our kids, safeguarding our health care workers, organizing volunteer drives for gloves and masks—none of this counts as part of "the economy," nor in any obvious way can this fetishized conception of the economy value the lives of those most at risk.

Disastrous leadership from the Trump administration and other Republican politicians has certainly made this pandemic much worse than it needed to be. But there were early missteps from Democrats too, including Bill DeBlasio, Andrew Cuomo, and later Gavin Newsom, who reopened California before he should have. Yet many of the features that have made COVID-19 so disruptive have much deeper roots in our political and social order. This is nowhere more apparent than in the structural features of our health care and public health sectors—features that make an effective response so difficult. Decades of neoliberal policies, supported by Democrats and Republicans alike, have installed a profit-driven health care system, a hyper-carceral approach to migration and social dislocation, an austerity-ravaged state that looks ever more like the neoliberal caricature, and a crisis of social reproduction. We continue to pay the price for those policies today.

As we continue fighting to bring this pandemic under control, it is imperative that we reject this neoliberal dispensation forcefully and head on. We must also embrace a broad-based vision of a new politics of care and work to change the crumbling structure of our broken society. We must build, in short, a new infrastructure of care to protect us all—a new order that, instead of perpetuating the virulent inequality and exploitation of late twentieth-century capitalism, makes health justice and care a core feature of our democracy.

IN ORDER TO ACHIEVE such a future, it is essential to understand how we got here. Today we lack anything that could be called a health care *system* because conservatives, insurers, and racists have done their utmost to block what most other industrialized countries have had for decades. Instead, we have a sea of different programs in which both the amount and quality of coverage are determined by who you are and where you live. This arrangement guarantees an inadequate national response to a national crisis—rather than one that is capable of coordination, of taking advantage of synergies, of sharing essential information on the number of cases, of disseminating guidelines on caring for the sick, and of allocating supplies and medicines rationally and equitably.

The health care we do provide has a laser-like focus on maximizing profit—one that has given us fewer hospital beds per capita than China, South Korea, and Italy, a paucity of primary care physicians, and a glut of overpriced specialists. Out-of-pocket costs for patients have grown steadily since the 1970s, averaging more than $1,000 per person in 2018. The average ER visit clocks in at around $500 in out-of-pocket costs. In addition, our system constantly produces new rules to extract surplus from the sick. (The latest are "surprise medical bills"—those that follow care in an in-network facility for services performed by an out-of-network provider, say an anesthesiologist, that can easily reach thousands or even tens of thousands of dollars for patients.) One in five Americans cannot pay their monthly bills in full, and 40 percent do not have the savings to cover an unexpected

$400 expense. Under these circumstances, any interaction with our health care system poses a grave financial risk to most Americans.

Then there are the uninsured. Around 27.5 million people were uninsured at the start of this pandemic, in part because of Republican attacks on the Affordable Care Act (ACA). Those fueled an 8.5 percent increase in the uninsured population since 2010. Conservatives worked hard to bring this about, always implying that the safety net they were shredding was for someone else—someone darker, far away, and less deserving. But as COVID-19 has proven, even those who think they can opt out by virtue of their wealth or status rely on the same public health infrastructure that keeps us *all* healthy and safe.

This is the essential logic of universal provision. While many European countries established some sort of compulsory health insurance at the end of the nineteenth century, the fight for universal health care in the United States has been an uphill battle. The American Medical Association and the health insurance industry have waged the opposition.

Efforts to expand health coverage across the United States have always encountered the country's deep commitment to racism, too. For instance, in the 1940s, southern Democrats conditioned their votes for the Hospital Survey and Construction Act on a rule that states be allowed to allocate resources locally, so that they could drive new hospital construction away from African American communities. Decades later, in 2012, when the Supreme Court willfully gutted the Affordable Care Act's provision mandating the expansion of Medicaid to low-income Americans, some states took advantage of this to deny their citizens health coverage that was 90 percent funded by the federal government. In these states, more than half of those who would have benefited from the expansion were people of color. A similar fact underlies decisions in some states under the Trump administration to institute work requirements and other barriers to health care.

Insurers, hospitals, and the pharmaceutical industry were always all in for a decentralized and weak system. A unified national system would give the state the power to bargain for lower costs, using its monopoly on care to face off against companies' monopolies on profit. It would also allow for the standardization of services—setting ceilings for charges for procedures and commodities—and for the evaluation of trade-offs between the costs and effectiveness of the interventions in our theoretically limitless "choice" of health care options. That choice, of course, is illusory for many.

Between February and May this year, 5.4 million Americans lost their health insurance because they lost their jobs. Our system of employer-based health care has never been so obviously deadly. Today COVID-19 is surging through the states that did not expand Medicaid, including Florida, Texas, and North Carolina. Nearly half of people laid off in those states also lost their health insurance. In July, in Nashville, a thirty-year-old African American man named Darius Settles died from COVID-19 five days after his diagnosis. He had twice visited the ER and returned home without being admitted. His father reported that he may have feared the medical bills he would have incurred: Darius had recently lost his health insurance after he lost his job in retail.

Darius Settles: say his name. His is just one story of unnecessary death and suffering as COVID-19 meets the U.S. health care paradox, a system that for all its technical excellence still leaves Americans dying younger than most of their contemporaries in the industrialized world.

WHY SHOULD THE ATTENDEES of Aspen, Davos, or the Conservative Political Action Conference—where several early, high-profile cases of COVID-19 were contracted—care about our fragmented and weak health care infrastructure? For one thing, it makes it more likely that hospitals around the country will be inundated with a wave of sickness, upending anyone in critical need of health care for COVID-19 or anything else. Exactly this situation unfolded in parts of Italy and in outbreak hotspots throughout the United States, such as New York. It is now playing out in new hotspots in Florida and Texas and in rural counties in states such as Kentucky and Ohio, which are seeing COVID-19 spikes from local meatpacking plants and prisons. Uninsured people who need care will have no primary care doctor to turn to and will belatedly present to overburdened ERs. States and localities are desperately scrambling to make plans to direct only those with the gravest illness to hospitals, knowing that they already face the prospect of an unmanageable surge in demand. Not only the uninsured but also many with insurance will likely delay care, presenting only when their cases become catastrophic.

People who cannot get early care will get sicker: more of them will need the ventilators, ICU beds, and the kind of advanced nursing care that had to be rationed in places such as Italy. And these delays in care mean more infectious people in our communities further spreading the virus rather than being in facilities that can care for them while isolating them from the uninfected.

This shambolic patchwork of a health care system, which purposefully disadvantages poor communities, communities of color, and immigrants, means millions affected by the outbreak are ineligible for care or facing economic hurdles to obtaining it. Undocumented immigrants are not eligible to use Medicaid or to purchase coverage through the ACA marketplaces. Under the new "public charge" rule, if immigrants receive Medicaid, they may jeopardize their chances of receiving a green card or other permanent status, creating a huge population of people who are discouraged or blocked from seeking care. Immigrants need to become "self-sufficient," the Trump administration announced when publishing the rule. This is quintessential neoliberalism—waving the Thatcherite flag that "people must look after themselves first," all the while building a structure to better extract labor from them as frontline workers after they've been cut loose from social support.

Then there are the implications of the austerity budgets of recent years. The groundwork for this kind of fiscal policy is bipartisan folly. Ever since Bill Clinton said in his 1996 State of the Union address that "the era of big government is over," Republicans and their centrist allies among the Democrats have made deficit reduction a bipartisan sign of prudence. This genuflection to fiscal conservatism as a marker of policy seriousness has had dire implications not just for the COVID-19 response but for the health of our society writ large. We have known since the work of Rudolf Virchow, who studied typhus in Upper Silesia in the mid-nineteenth century, and Friedrich Engels, who studied the conditions of the English working class, that we create conditions that make people sick, and that those who lack economic, social, and political power typically bear the greatest burden of disease. More recent work on the impact of inequality on health reveals another truth: inequality is *itself* associated with poorer health outcomes, including lower life expectancies across nations. The austerity of the last four decades, and the skyrocketing inequality that has accompanied it, have deeply degraded the health of U.S. society.

As just one example, consider the agency ostensibly in charge of protecting our nation from threats like the one we now face. Funding for the U.S. Centers for Disease Control and Prevention (CDC) has decreased by 10 percent over the past decade. Meanwhile 17 states and the District of Columbia have cut their health budgets over the past few years, and 20 percent of local health departments have followed. Over 55,000 jobs at local health departments have been lost since 2008. Yet when Trump was asked in a press conference on February 26 whether the COVID-19 crisis had given him pause over his administration's cuts to the CDC, National Institutes of Health (NIH), and World Health Organization (WHO), he downplayed the implications of retrenchment. "Some of the people we cut, they haven't been used for many, many years," he replied. "You know, I'm a business person, I don't like having thousands of people around when you don't need 'em. When we need 'em we can get 'em back very quickly."

Furthermore, the CDC's Public Health Emergency Preparedness (PHEP) program, the key financing mechanism for state and local public health emergency preparedness, has been cut by a third since

2003. To make matters worse, the president's 2021 proposed budget slashes $25 million from the Office of Public Health Preparedness and Response, $18 million from the Hospital Preparedness Program, and $85 million from the Emerging and Zoonotic Infectious Diseases program. All of this underscores a bipartisan trend to underfund our nation's public health in the name of deficit and debt reduction.

As the fortunes of federal, state, and local public health programs have suffered under both parties over the past few decades, the role of expertise in government has split them. Many note the regressive politics of neoliberal technocracy, which pushes bold, structural reforms aside for technical tweaks and fixes. But there are parts of the state that necessitate expertise, especially public health.

The degradation of expertise in the Trump administration has indeed been catastrophic. There are experts ready to act—many of the career civil servants at the CDC's headquarters in Atlanta are superb public health physicians, scientists, and practitioners—but the administration's course on COVID-19 was more responsive to a president worried about reelection than to a virus killing its citizens. Most of the appointed health officials in the administration, from Health and Human Services (HHS) secretary Alex Azar to Surgeon General Jerome Adams, have emerged as cheerleaders and sycophants, aiding and abetting the disinformation coming from the White House by refusing to correct the president's errors in real time. Others, such as Ambassador Deborah Birx and HHS assistant secretary Brett Giroir, have treated the crisis as a career opportunity, denigrating line staff at the CDC and pushing rival scientists such as NIH's Anthony Fauci to the sidelines in a quest for more personal influence and power in the White House. Finally, President Trump's withdrawal from the WHO compounds this disaster—the pandemic is a global phenomenon requiring international cooperation on data collection, research, and the development of interventions, not scientific isolationism by fiat.

The basic ideology of U.S. governance also works against the best scientific response when it comes to treatments and vaccines. Drug prices have spiraled out of control because the United States lacks any systematic means to control them. This too is no accident. President Barack Obama decided that he needed Big Pharma as an industry ally, so refused to take it on during the ACA fight. When Medicare expanded drug coverage, the industry extracted a provision that forbids the government from negotiating prices. Measures such as generic competition, which can be invoked under existing law if the administration were serious about bringing the industry to heel, could bring prices down. But they are not being used. Under pressure from industry, the FDA also refuses to share clinical trial data from companies with researchers and the public, even where it has clear value: data that, for example, identifies COVID-19–related drug shortages, or that would help us verify the results of drug safety and efficacy tests conducted by industries that stand to gain billions from the results.

All of these conditions are byproducts of a system organized by an insatiable concern with profit and infected with a reflexive suspicion of the government—even though government is the only mechanism that we have to invest in the long-term tools that we need to protect us in a pandemic.

WHERE DO WE GO from here? Our answer must connect to a broader politics that addresses the deep structural roots of the problems we face in the United States. We must build for a better future, not just climb out of the rubble of this pandemic, brush ourselves off, and return to business as usual. We need a new politics of care, one organized around a commitment to universal provision for human needs; countervailing power for workers, people of color, and the vulnerable; and a rejection of carceral approaches to social problems. The question now is how to connect that vision to programmatic responses that address the needs of the moment and beyond. We need to aim at "non-reformist reforms"—reforms that embody a vision of the different world we want, and that work from a theory of power-building that recognizes that real change requires changing who has a say in our political process.

The proposals from the progressive wing of the Democratic Party, and even those from democratic socialists, are missing what we might call a New Deal for Public Health. Here, social movements are indispensable. In particular, the AIDS movement of the past forty years offers a template for the kinds of mobilization we'll need to achieve our goals: not only bringing the virus under control, but also building a future where something like this never happens again.

What might that include? The Medicare for All component has been mapped out, but less obvious and just as crucial is a new, robust, long-lasting infrastructure of care. For example, people need to be able to stay home when they are sick. Yet employment in this country systematically undermines our ability to care for ourselves and others. Women have it the worst, especially immigrant women and women of color, for they are the ones with the highest burdens of paid and unpaid care. The truth is stark: more than 32 million workers lack access to paid sick days. While 93 percent of the highest-wage workers have access to paid sick days, only 30 percent of the lowest-wage workers do. The risk of job loss and precarious scheduling all add to employees' difficulties. Without anything like universal sick pay or income insurance, self-employed and gig economy workers are cast adrift at a time like this.

The risk is extraordinary for those who are caring for others—the fast food workers and orderlies and nursing home workers who have had no choice but to continue to work. And because they care for us, their risk is also ours. We already know that paid sick leave slows the spread of epidemics such as influenza. Other kinds of social support—food and rental assistance, too—are essential in a pandemic, when ordinary forms of income may be unavailable. Temporary measures like these will help, but it is broader social support that is needed in the long term—not just to combat this pandemic, but also to address the burden of health inequity and chronic disease in this country. The social safety net that Republicans and neoliberal Democrats love to hate is what undergirds successful health systems; rebuilding it will be the foundation of a New Deal for Public Health.

The United States has shunted millions of people out of the circle of care—casting them out, like the immigrants being rounded up by Immigration and Customs Enforcement; locking them up, like the millions of incarcerated men and women in our prisons and jails; or throwing them on the street, like the hundreds of thousands of people without a home. These are among the most vulnerable. Immigrants won't come forward for care if they fear deportation. Those in our prisons and jails are at significant risk of infection. Many, if not most, of the homeless have nowhere to go; the few homeless shelters are woefully unprepared to handle such a crisis. As Anand Giridharadas warned earlier this year: "Your health is as safe as that of the worst-insured, worst-cared-for person in your society. It will be decided by the height of the floor, not the ceiling." Unless we bring everyone into the circle of care in the United States, we will all be vulnerable. COVID-19 has shone a light on the cruelty of life in the United States. We cannot look away now.

The impact of our fight against COVID-19 on workers, the poor, and retirement savings is real. It is essential that we address these human needs. This pandemic is a long-term epidemiological and economic event. But conventional wisdom is still mistaking the current moment for something akin to the 2007–8 financial crisis—a rupture that needs a "stimulus." Despite the headlong charge to reopen around the country, it is clear we are going to have to consider additional lockdowns and extended periods of social distancing. Our leaders still haven't understood this vital fact: until we get the virus under control, our economy cannot be put back online. We haven't learned from our counterparts around the world: we don't need to be turbo-charging our economy right now. We need, instead, to put it on pause until we can drive new cases down to levels we're seeing elsewhere. Only then can we reasonably think of opening up as other countries have begun to do. This is what Germany and other nations did, yet we think we can power through the pandemic by force of wishful thinking rather than putting in place the policies we need to survive.

We need a surge of support so that we can get through to the other end of this pandemic with the least damage. This doesn't mean the indiscriminate tax cuts and bailouts for the corporate class that we saw in spring 2020. It means supporting all of those who cannot get through this pandemic without help. That is hundreds of millions of Americans, and if we triage assistance, it's those most in need who need to be at the front of the line. We should prioritize interventions that meet people's basic needs for social reproduction—to protect housing, to ensure that people can sustain themselves and their families through this ongoing shock, and to provide extra care for all of the workers essential to the response.

Income is also critical for the millions who will not be reached by employment-based support, including gig workers, the self-employed, small businesses, and the long-term unemployed. Ordinary Americans need broader relief as well. Early on, the Trump administration made some moves to temporarily prevent evictions and foreclosures, and banks and non-bank lenders made proposals for broader moratoria on home loan payments, requiring tens of billions of dollars in federal guarantees. Localities and states took action to protect renters in some places, but those measures are coming to an end, leading many to warn of an impending eviction apocalypse. No one can shelter in place without a home. We need an urgent plan to prevent evictions, and not just defer but cancel rent, so that families are not buried under a wave of debt once temporary moratoria expire. One-off payments to individuals and debt deferral have not gotten us to where we need to be: in a position to shelter in place safely, together, until we get the pandemic under control.

The right way to look at the tradeoff isn't in terms of potential losses in GDP versus the benefits of averting illness and death. In that cold calculus of efficiency, those at highest risk of complications from COVID-19, for example the elderly and the infirm, seem expendable. But in human terms, this means a sacrifice of our parents and grandparents and our neighbors, by the hundreds of thousands. This is worse than the specter of "death panels" that conservatives fabricated to protect Americans from too much health care. It is a death drive, and the driver is capitalism.

WHAT WE NEED is not unprecedented. The United States has made great social investments in times of crisis, from the New Deal here at home to the post–World War II Marshall Plan abroad. As a country, we once decided to rescue citizens from the rubble of catastrophe and help them build a health system. Instead of relaxing social distancing and other disease control measures, we must consider instead how to ramp up a Public Works for Public Health program, and a new politics of care that can help us meet the challenge of COVID-19 and build a deeper democracy along the way.

Care means much more than contact tracing and exposure notification. We need to direct resources to frontline clinics and hospitals in Florida, Texas, and Arizona, but we must also be alert to needs elsewhere as new waves of the virus wash over us this fall and winter. We also need to quickly expand our health care capacity, for example by asking the recently retired to come back to the workforce, as has been done in New York City, and finding new places to offer hospital beds and care for the mildly sick.

We must also do all we can to facilitate the development of safe, effective, and affordable drugs and vaccines. Here, too, the path forward is through the public. As in all pandemics, the public will lead in funding the response, and is already pouring billions of dollars into vaccine development, much of it routed through private companies. The government should demand that companies that succeed also agree to a reasonable price for any cures or vaccines, and share knowledge with others so that suppliers can emerge to meet world, not just U.S., needs. We must also require that companies share the clinical trial data that sustain their claims; today, much of it is hidden by corporate secrecy. We need public information about research and development costs to negotiate fair prices for things that work. As importantly, we must not succumb to the fantasy that a cure lies just around the corner.

This wish for deliverance is part of the emotional texture of suffering, but it can undermine support for the systems that ensure that the drugs we are using actually work. As longtime AIDS activists, we know this personally from the early HIV epidemic, when people were grasping at straws trying anything from egg lipid concoctions to blood thinners to save their own lives and the lives of their friends. It took over a decade to find a set of drugs that actually worked to beat back the virus and finally reduce deaths. Yet our president has broadcast unapproved cures that jeopardize citizens' health. The sad tale of hydroxychloroquine—its ceaseless promotion by the president and cronies such as Peter Navarro—has distracted from our task. Drug development by presidential whim or baseless enthusiasm generated by company press releases will not help: without evidence of what works, we will waste our efforts chasing dead ends rather than expediting rigorous research.

While federal action is critical, there is much that can be done at state and local levels. Close to home, we need our leaders to protect those who cannot social distance because they are in our prisons and jails or living on the street or in homeless shelters. This is where social solidarity is most needed and most in short supply. In correctional facilities, the close quarters and unsanitary conditions make the campaign against COVID-19 a losing game. Moreover, the elderly population in prisons is growing: close to 30,000 inmates in state and federal prisons in the United States are over sixty-five, and this group is especially vulnerable to complications and death from COVID-19. Additionally, infections that spread in prisons commonly spread to the communities around them: viruses don't respect prison walls.

Advocates for the incarcerated have called for the release of elderly prisoners and those at high risk of disease, to protect these individuals and to keep these places from amplifying transmission. In some places, judges have begun to see the dangers, and have ordered releases. The ACLU and others are working to obtain the release of people in immigration detention, who are also in danger. Scaling this up will require action from politicians. So far both Democrats and Republicans have resisted, hanging on to the ruthless dictates of the pre-pandemic world even as they enact measures to protect those beyond the grip of our carceral state. Thus far, ten of the largest clusters (more than a thousand cases each) of COVID-19 in the United States are in prisons, jails, and detention facilities. Looking tough on crime is no substitute for sound public health policies.

Homeless men and women are in another predicament. While being on the streets exposes them to many dangers and health risks, the group settings of many homeless shelters put them at high risk of acquiring COVID-19. The homeless are also increasingly elderly and sick, which again puts them at greater risk of death from COVID-19. Early on, localities explored repurposing schools and other public buildings to appropriately house homeless individuals in the context of the pandemic, but they were met with resistance from communities. Many of those programs are now expiring or being retracted. We need a long-term solution to safely house the homeless because this virus is not going away, and nor is the need. Because many people experiencing homelessness are also suffering from mental illness and addiction, housing solutions also need to be combined with care and treatment for these conditions—for instance, offering psychiatric medications and opioid agonist therapy—to help them cope with their new surroundings and the restrictions of social distancing.

Data has shown that, during this pandemic, domestic abuse has become "more frequent, more severe and more dangerous" and that mental health and substance abuse issues are on the rise. We cannot just walk away from these people, our neighbors in crisis. In the narrowest sense, ignoring these needs will make it harder for people to keep social distancing. In a broader sense, if we use our politics at a time of existential need to impose an unlivable life on our fellow citizens—if we fail those for whom staying at home might be more dangerous than the virus—we will tear away at the fabric of solidarity and trust that we need to maintain the shared project that is democracy.

Right now we're leaving help with all of this largely to individuals, families, and voluntary support. Most of us know people who are cutting corners with social distancing because they just cannot meet their daily needs any other way. While the mutual aid networks springing up around the country can handle a few requests for support, as we scale up testing and contact tracing, the need of these kinds of social services and economic aid will explode. This cannot be handled simply as a matter of volunteerism, even if, as Mike Konczal has written, "conservatives dream of returning to a world where private charity fulfilled all public needs."

It is essential to recognize that while COVID-19 has cut its deadly swath from coast to coast, the disease has followed the same patterns of inequality we've always seen embedded in the U.S. landscape, where the death rate for predominantly African American counties is sixfold higher than in predominantly white counties, and where this crisis is just heaped upon others that have been plaguing these communities for generations.

Meanwhile, as millions of Americans continue to stay home in solidarity with their neighbors, the economic contraction has come at a great cost, dragging families and individuals to the brink in the most spectacular economic collapse since the 1930s. We remain in the middle of a disaster scene today, aided and abetted by a political culture that gave corporations billions in bailouts but hung ordinary people out to dry. Food pantries are running empty as farmers—themselves facing bankruptcy—plow their crops into the soil. Poorer families and school districts don't have the resources for online learning, meaning that we are leaving millions of kids behind. Rent strikes are popping up from coast to coast.

We also need to address the explosion of infections in the workplace. We've seen outbreaks, large and small, in meat processing plants across the country, in Amazon warehouses and Walmarts, leading to walkouts and lawsuits. As more businesses reopen, employees and employers need help to keep themselves and their customers safe. Areas for employees and customers must be reconfigured to maximize social distancing and new workplace protocols need to be developed. Employers should be held responsible for taking the steps needed to protect their workers and the public, and some of this will likely not come without a stronger role for labor—via labor-management commissions, for example. An infection control brigade could work in cooperation with employees and employers, advising them on best practices, and ensuring that supplies of personal protective equipment—from masks to gloves to physical barriers like plexiglass shields for cashiers—are available. They could also ensure that early signs of failures in infection control are discovered and addressed immediately.

IT IS CLEAR, then, that following public health advice to stay home and socially distance isn't as easy as it sounds—and its costs do not fall evenly. We need to support people to undertake this act of solidarity. We also need a new cadre of care workers who can provide specific help to individuals infected and affected by COVID-19, to enable them to follow public health and medical advice. In other words, if the health infrastructure we need should come in the form of a New Deal for Public Health, then the crisis response team we need should come from a massive new jobs program: call it the Community Health Corps. Funded federally and organized locally, it would put millions of Americans to work caring for one another, and with larger goals than just beginning to turn around the unemployment figures we see today. It would serve our needs for a vast force that can track and trace the virus, while adding workers who can help support those in need, secure our health, and build solidarity among us.

COVID-19 is not the only health crisis facing many communities across the United States. Reducing this effort to a telephone call to notify someone of their exposure to SARS-CoV-2 ignores the health disparities that existed before 2020 and set the stage for the disproportionate impact we see in communities of color now from COVID-19. Even if our only aim were to contain the pandemic, COVID-19 is racing through many communities so quickly that testing and exposure notification are insufficient to stem the tide of the pandemic. We'll need a wider set of approaches to help people stay safe, navigate the pandemic, practice social distancing and infection control, and deal with the social and economic pressures that will make this difficult for many Americans. This new Community Health Corps can take on these larger tasks, to start rebuilding the health of our communities from the ground up. COVID-19 may be the priority now, but we can't wait to tackle the other health threats that put us at such risk. Such a broad-based program, operating in rural and urban areas around the country, could help us weather this pandemic, prepare for future ones, and mitigate the cataclysmic employment dislocation of the coming months and years.

In truth, this is just a new form of an old idea—a Works Progress Administration (WPA) for an age of pandemics. But the aim is larger: to bring us through the crisis by calling into being government as we wish it to be—caring for us, bringing us together, while also enabling us to live our different lives. It would go beyond providing care to communities, stitching back together the personal connections torn asunder by our self-enforced isolation and building power together, as workers and patients are tied to each other through the act of caregiving. It wouldn't just create jobs to fill a hole during the crisis—it would develop skills and foster solidarity that will form the basis of the post-crisis economy, too.

We are already seeing small steps in this direction. Massachusetts asked Partners in Health (PiH), which has experience building community health workforces in places hit by disease and disaster around the globe, to spearhead its contact tracing program. In a matter of weeks, PiH hired and trained close to a thousand people for these important and complex jobs. Aware of the importance of the work and the demands of the job, PiH is paying them the same rate as U.S. Census takers, $27 an hour, providing them with health insurance, and prioritizing hiring the unemployed and people of color. About 17,000 applied for these jobs, showing that there is a deep pool of people willing to do this work. That should come as no surprise, given the staggering rate of unemployment, the inadequacy of government assistance, and the outpouring of support we've seen in communities. People want to help. We just need to organize them.

The problem is, while these efforts are admirable, state-level programs are vastly underfunded and overreliant on volunteers. Before the crisis, public health departments employed fewer than 2,000 contact tracers in the country. The best early estimate projected that we would need to hire as many as 300,000 of them to address this outbreak. A recent piece of legislation proposed by Senators Kirsten Gillibrand and Michael Bennet suggested we needed a million people across the country to take on contact tracing, but also the larger work of rebuilding health in our communities as we described above.

We also have models for how this work can be done. One such model derives from so-called community health worker (CHW) programs, which have a long history in the United States and around the world. Today, we have about 120,000 community health care workers in places around the country doing health education and prevention work, collecting data, and making links between local residents and the services they need. They are most often from the underserved communities they work in. Local CHWs can help to make care accessible and establish trust.

There are also models for the caseworker and legal support component in the medical-legal partnerships (MLPs) that have emerged around the country in recent years. Driven by the recognition that illness and health care costs are shaped by factors out of doctors' control (like access to safe housing and benefits), hospitals and nonprofits around the country have hired legal professionals to assist clinicians, social workers, and case managers in addressing structural issues affecting patients' health and well-being. As of early 2019, there were MLPs active in about 330 hospitals and health centers in 46 states. There is evidence that MLPs can improve patient health outcomes, benefit mental health, remove barriers to health care for low-income families, and increase access to stable housing.

We should work to build on these successes, which operate in small and disjointed ways, by integrating them into a federally funded WPA for the age of COVID-19. It will require significant federal funding, especially as states are forced into austerity by plummeting tax revenues and balanced budget requirements. But the cost will be small compared to the $2 trillion stimulus. Even a vastly larger program, hiring 5 million Americans for the duration of the crisis, would still cost less than the corporate bailout. This is a deal, if we consider what it can do to save lives, employ people, and buffer against economic depression.

We could also mold the program to help those who are at grave risk, but not of dying from COVID-19. Many young people today are facing a terrifying future. With more than 26 million unemployed, who will hire someone fresh from high school? How will students get their first job to pay off their college loans? Young people are least likely to develop serious complications from COVID-19, making them an obvious priority for a jobs program. We also should demand a program that hires those who are hardest hit by this downturn.

This means looking beyond workers who are already highly skilled. Some of these recruits will need significant training, but we should not think of that as a problem—these are the same jobs we will need after COVID-19, and we have chronic shortages of exactly those skills. And many of these jobs will use skills that come quickly: those who will deliver food, masks, and hand sanitizer can be trained in days.

We know from those who study the impact of jobs guarantees—including programs that have been running for many years in other countries—that such programs can be scaled up quickly, provide essential counter-cyclical stability, and discipline the private labor market. Especially now, creating alternatives to exploitative jobs is urgent, the only right thing to do. Many "essential jobs"—janitors, cashiers, delivery workers—look a lot like forced labor today. With few exceptions, if you quit, you aren't eligible for unemployment. Other forms of support, such as those elusive $1,200 checks, are too small and widely unavailable. A Community Health Corps could provide better jobs, driving up the pay of those workers whom we call essential but pay badly. If these corps jobs stick around (folded in, perhaps, to a Medicare for All program), they can help address our needs for care and our needs for decent work. We can also build the corps as a springboard for further training, where those who have served their country can be funneled into higher education, in a new GI Bill for the age of COVID-19.

The United States may have the most technologically advanced health care system in the world, but we're the epicenter of the pandemic because we've badly trailed other industrialized nations in health outcomes for years. Many of the hardest-hit communities have been reeling from long-term health crises: the opioid epidemic and deaths of despair in Appalachia, the burden of maternal deaths and the ongoing HIV epidemic in the South, an explosion of obesity across the country. The United States is sicker now with COVID-19, but we've been sick for a long while in many other ways.

Beyond helping to manage the current crisis, then, a Community Health Corps would help to improve the health of people historically excluded from the circle of care. For too long we've focused on funding expensive, technologically advanced specialty care, while neglecting primary and community care and underpaying caregivers. Even in the midst of the pandemic, community health centers, which should be the core of our health approach, have teetered on financial ruin. Meanwhile, domestic workers and home health aides have been underpaid and left out of federal labor protections. Not to mention that much of the work of caring is still done at home, falling disproportionately on women and people of color.

Shoring up the foundations of U.S. health care by valuing care itself isn't just the first step toward a more rapid, effective response to health threats in the future. It will also move us toward a new politics of care that starts from the ground up, in the places we live, work, and socialize. It will be a politics that builds power among caregivers, as the act of caring itself becomes publicly recognized and compensated for the productive work it is. Done right—and without the racialized and gendered exclusions that characterized the WPA—these new jobs can be a source of power for those who have never been fully allowed a voice in our democracy.

To scale this up quickly, we will need to bring together organizations that are experienced at mobilizing locally while being attentive to civil, social, and economic rights. Examples include Partners in Health, the Center for Popular Democracy, and Community Change, Inc.

OVER THE PAST FOUR DECADES, we've seen the erosion of government as a force for good in people's lives, as conservatives have moved to weaken its effectiveness and privatize its functions. Liberals have gone along and lost their faith in the kind of government that built their political base while helping millions in the modern era, starting with the New Deal and the social and economic programs that defined the Great Society period in the 1960s. The U.S. state is so weak and untrusted now that banks have had to take over as the vehicle for the provision of many of the billions released under emergency appropriations by Congress.

A Community Health Corps could be part of the remedy by renewing faith in government's ability to help. The corps would also be a prophylaxis—a first line in the response to the next challenges we face, whether it's a seasonal return of COVID-19, another pandemic, or the monumental troubles that climate change will soon rain down.

We need more than a jobs program at this moment of national crisis, to be sure. We also need income replacement and the comprehensive action that we've described as a New Deal for Public Health. But rising up from under the cruel weight of this pandemic, we should also look ahead and configure new programs, like a Community Health Corps. Such a corps can be a model for a Green New Deal jobs program for the looming health crisis of climate change. Getting back to normal was never going to be a solace for many in our country. Business as usual is precisely what has made us vulnerable to disasters like this.

Will it be easy to get our creaking democracy to funnel resources into these programs? Probably not. But COVID-19 is showing us that care—broadly conceived—is central to a healthy society. Rudolf Virchow, the father of social medicine, once said:

> Medicine is a social science and politics is nothing else but medicine on a large scale. Medicine as a social science, as the science of human beings, has the obligation to point out problems and to attempt their theoretical solution; the politician . . . must find the means for their actual solution.

Together with a broad-based movement for a new infrastructure of care in the United States, a Community Health Corps is one solution, one place to start to build a new movement that heals us and our body politic, and that will allow us—all of us—to survive a pandemic, and, then, to thrive.

IN
THIS
TOGETHER

ETHICS AT A DISTANCE

Vafa Ghazavi

AS WE SAT DOWN FOR DINNER in late April 2020, the windows of our Oxford apartment started rattling. Outside, the street was erupting in applause as neighbors put their hands—and their tin pots—together for the UK's National Health Service. We threw open our windows and joined the din for what is now a weekly national ritual during the pandemic. I thought of our city's hospital, where a friend works in emergency. With a little pride, I also thought of my mother back in Australia, an Iranian refugee who worked for decades as a registered nurse.

The gesture of gratitude was symbolic, of course. It was another reminder of how Janus-faced the fight is: individuated, tiny acts binding us to our collective fate. The only way to beat it, experts say, is to "flatten the curve." By slowing its spread, we can buy time for health systems to get it under control, including by increasing ICU capacity and upping the supply of ventilators and protective equipment.

In many places where the health crisis is acute, the importance of individual action has gone from widely dismissed to an article of faith. Hand washing. Coughing into your elbow. Restricting activities outside your home. These ordinary, everyday acts now have vast human, political, and economic ramifications. The implications of what seemed trivial a few weeks ago now reach to the heights of geopolitics and the rise and fall of nations. The core responsibility of each person has a strangely paradoxical character: the social thing to do is to isolate yourself. In an unusually explicit way, the virus makes salient the power of a single person.

Philosophers are among those who have written about the ethics of small actions that have large consequences. Perhaps the most well-known example comes from Derek Parfit. In *Reasons and Persons* (1984), he compares two thought experiments. In one case, there are a thousand torturers, each of whom controls an electronic torture device connected to one victim. Each device features a dial with a thousand settings controlling the level of pain imparted. The pain imparted by each turn of the dial is imperceptible, but if the dial is turned all the way up, the victim experiences severe agony. And everyone would agree that if each torturer turns the dial a thousand times, each torturer has committed a great moral wrong by imparting severe agony.

In the other scenario, Parfit imagines the same pain being imparted but in a way that makes no one torturer responsible for imparting any perceptible pain at all. In this case, each of the torturers presses a button, which turns all thousand dials one time, but none of them know what the others are doing. After each torturer presses the button, the victims suffer in total the same amount of pain as in the first case, but now none of the individual torturers has caused pain in any of the victims. The harm is diffused rather than localized; the torturers are "harmless."

The moral problem posed by this thought experiment has less to do with the quantification of harm and more with how humans cut themselves off from the consequences of their actions. And as we better understand our capacity to spread the virus—when we get our heads around the possibility that we might be asymptomatic vectors, for example, passing it on via a surface we touch in the grocery store—such analogies have diminishing relevance. Harmless torturers—that is, each of us—can't be deemed harmless once we know how our actions are linked to the suffering of others, even if it remains difficult to acknowledge our destructive role due to a significant dose of bias.

THE IDEA THAT WE ARE CONNECTED to the harm of others in subtle and fragmented ways lies behind many pressing ethical challenges. Some philosophers have tried to make the case for why we are morally compelled to respond to our entanglement using complicated chains of harm.

In his aptly named book, *Complicity* (2000), Christopher Kutz, for example, suggests that we should each be held accountable for willfully participating in collective activity that causes harm (not merely instances where we cause harm directly). Likewise, Judith Lichtenberg writes in *Distant Strangers* (2014) about the "new harms" of our globalized world that are "seamlessly woven into our normal routines." We buy cell phones that use coltan mined by warlords and fill our cars with fuel that enriches despots. We eat shrimp farmed by modern-day slaves and chocolate made from cocoa harvested by children. We wear jeans manufactured by exploited women in sweatshops. The anthropologist Mary L. Gray worries that a new global underclass is emerging due to ubiquitous digital platforms that use artificial intelligence but only function with human "ghost work" such as data labeling and content moderation.

Many of our interactions with the world, it turns out, connect us to the suffering of others while at the same time psychologically distancing us from them. Through our normalized action, we risk becoming cogs in a machine without seeing what the machine is producing—components in Parfit's torture device, rather than its controller. The deep moral problem, then, is a narrowing of structural vision, rather than a failure to account for individuated wrongdoing. We do a distinct kind of wrong when we refuse to notice social structures that co-opt us in elevating some while subordinating others. We mistakenly substitute a focus on individuated blame for what should be a concern for the common good.

The critical ethical challenge is to render the relationship between individual agency and structural change more perspicuous. Political theorist Melissa Lane points out in *Eco-Republic* (2012) how hard it is for humans to understand their actions as anything other than negligible in the face of large social problems. But, more hopefully, she also stresses how it is possible to do so by cultivating our political imagination. Lane applies her thinking to the climate crisis. The ripple effects of our seemingly negligible individual actions may be easier to perceive during COVID-19 than the climate crisis, but the demands on political imagination right now might be harder—the pandemic has been thrust upon us without the benefit of an intense process of social learning leading into it.

Lane's argument cuts in two directions. The problem is not just that we fail to appreciate the full effects of our actions, but also that the sense of our own negligibility can make us feel powerless to contribute to badly needed social transformation. It is easy to be defeated by a sort of Zeno's paradox of moral resignation: if we think no step we take can move us forward, we fail to act. Lane defuses the problem by insisting that significant social change *can* be brought about by what might look like negligible steps, with each human node shifting the parameters of political possibility—just as, contrary to Zeno, we are not destined to remain motionless. In particular, Lane argues, uncertainty and unpredictability reign in politics and human action, so it is a mistake to assume these domains operate within a stable equilibrium. Social models that presuppose humans don't have the capacity for collective action because of a fixed or ingrained set of interests, habits, or identities run the risk of fulfilling their own predictions.

CONSIDERED IN THIS LIGHT, the pandemic is a high-stakes version of an older, deeper challenge to take steps to build a world that more fully recognizes our overlapping fate. Acknowledging our complicity in the harm of others, or sharpening our sense of who to blame, is not a sure enough foundation for that kind of moral work. Culpability doesn't inspire civic virtues of steadfastness or sacrifice. One need not go as far as Barbara Fried and reject the idea of blame altogether in order to recognize that the disposition to blame others can become an obstacle to solving societal problems. Indeed, when it turns into a pattern of targeting the most vulnerable among us for structural failures, such blame typifies the spiritual and intellectual impoverishment of our age.

In contrast to the backward-looking nature of blame, realizing the power of one person can orient us to the future. This involves taking up what political theorist Iris Marion Young in *Responsibility for Justice* (2012) calls a "social connection model" of responsibility that focuses on eliminating the background conditions of structural injustice. Each of us must seek an individual commitment to find creative ways to make and remake norms and institutions so they can better protect all people, especially the most vulnerable, from threats of domination or marginalization, including those compounded by a health emergency or economic collapse. That includes not just the nurses and doctors we clap for, not just teachers and farmers, but also all the precariously employed and unemployed, from the postal workers, janitors, and grocery clerks who can't afford to self-isolate, to all those performing the work of care. And this commitment shouldn't be restricted by borders, even if it is mostly mediated through local and national initiatives.

This moral work is really that of a joint project among many. It is less about the harm we might inflict through our everyday interactions, and more about the capacity of ordinary citizens to create a just social order through social action and participation in conversations about the moral basis of collective life. Contrary to the logic that says small steps are futile, each person has a part to play in that project, harnessing the diversity of wisdom, talents, roles, and social circumstances found in society at large. Flipping the script from spectatorship to agency is vital for addressing the present crisis as well as properly learning its lessons.

If we enrich our political imagination deeply enough, we will invest in the social and economic infrastructure needed to realize the widely espoused but poorly enacted idea that every person has equal moral worth. Each of us bears some responsibility for making that happen—in our daily encounters, in the life of our communities, and in other efforts we take up, however slight they may seem, to shape the direction of society as a whole.

LOVE ONE ANOTHER OR DIE

Amy Hoffman

INSTEAD OF VIEWING Donald Trump's daily barrage of fantasies and lies about COVID-19 as unprecedented and shocking, we should perhaps see it simply as business as usual. Ignore it, cover it up, and wish it away. While hundreds of thousands suffer and die. It's all too familiar.

The Great Communicator, Ronald Reagan—who was president from the beginnings of the AIDS epidemic through its horrifying, unchecked spread—notoriously failed to even utter the word AIDS in public until 1987. And before he finally deigned to mention it, and no doubt after as well, the disease was treated around his West Wing as a hilarious fag joke.

Social distancing in my apartment during today's terrifying pandemic has given me time to reflect on the early days of queer liberation and that other pandemic. In particular, I have thought about how, when celebrating the fiftieth anniversary of Stonewall in June 2019, we committed a grave error by not making the HIV/AIDS crisis a central feature of our recollections.

While it's too simplistic to speak in terms of lessons that can be transcribed from HIV/AIDS onto COVID-19, I believe we can benefit in general from recalling what it was like to live as a community under siege, and how we rose to the challenge of caring for one another. In the following, which draws heavily on my own memory, I recall what LGBTQ life was like in the first decades following the Stonewall riots, and how that determined our response to a plague.

IT IS IMPOSSIBLE to understand the lives of queer people in the 1950s and '60s without talking about the bars. The old species of gay bar, of which the Stonewall Inn was an example, does not exist anymore. These bars were usually owned by the mafia, even when they were managed by queers. The management would pay off the police in order to prevent raids, although raids happened anyway, and sometimes the police just came in and swaggered around, to make sure everyone felt sufficiently threatened. In some, if you weren't actively drinking you could be ejected; in some, touching was forbidden. Strange liquor license regulations limited behavior: in New York City, bars that served "homosexuals" simply were not granted liquor licenses, so all of their operations were illegal, at least on paper; in Boston, blue laws forbade dancing after midnight. (Even in the late 1970s, I remember police invading The Saints lesbian bar and turning off the jukebox. We all gathered around and stared at them, hoping we looked intimidating. We didn't.) Traditionally, bar patrons were required to be wearing at least three items of clothing of the "appropriate" sex or face arrest. People of color, femme gay men, all lesbians (whom the bartenders said didn't drink or tip enough), and generally nonconforming people were harassed, discriminated against, and banned.

For all the policing the bars faced, they were often overcrowded firetraps. In a 1973 arson fire at the UpStairs Lounge in New Orleans, thirty-two people died, unable to escape the second-floor club. And in 1977, a blaze at the Everard Baths in Manhattan killed nine patrons and decimated the building (although enough of it was still usable for the bathhouse to continue operating until 1986, when Mayor Ed Koch shut it down in an attempt to slow the AIDS epidemic). Gay bars were also filthy. The mafia-owned Stonewall Inn had no running water. Dishes and glassware were "cleaned" by a swish through a basin of indescribable liquid. During the riot, when the police, trapped inside the bar, attempted to disperse the crowd by hosing them—in imitation of Sheriff Bull Connor's actions against civil rights protesters in Birmingham, Alabama—all they got was a ridiculously symbolic dribble.

Gay bars were often located in dangerous or obscure neighborhoods, where queerbashers could easily attack the patrons as they came or went, or even invade the bars and beat people up. In Boston, The Saints was in the financial district, which was deserted at night. The multiracial lesbian collective that ran it would try to make sure women didn't leave alone, and if a patron had too much to drink, they would find someone to escort them home. A nice policy, but it didn't prevent lesbian-haters from waylaying and beating up unprotected women. Men in cruising areas such as Boston's Fenway Victory

Gardens risked attack, and taking home the wrong trick from a bar could be fatal. One of my friends on the staff of Boston's weekly *Gay Community News*, Mel Horne, was mugged and stabbed to death as he and his boyfriend reeled home after spending an evening drinking at the gay bar Chaps.

So for safety reasons, queer bars did not have signs or a street presence. You had to know where they were. At *Gay Community News*, we did not publish the address of The Saints—we only gave it out to women who were enough in the know to call and ask for it. And I never figured out how anyone knew the name of the Beacon Hill gay bar Sporters—or for that matter, how they knew it existed at all, behind a façade that appeared to be boarded up and deserted.

The policing of LGBTQ people's lives was not confined to the bars, of course. Lesbians, especially, often met at private house parties—there is a wonderful description of such a party in Audre Lorde's biomythography *Zami: A New Spelling of My Name* (1982). If you weren't discreet enough—or even if you were, but had, say, an angry neighbor or a disgruntled ex—the parties could be raided too. According to Justin Spring's 2010 biography *Secret Historian*, gay tattoo artist and sexual adventurer Samuel Steward decorated his apartment in the 1950s with his erotic drawings and photographs of gay men. Seeing this, his tricks would often be not just appalled but terrified. Even though the artwork was in Steward's private home, they knew he could be (and eventually was) arrested and jailed for creating and displaying such works.

I'm recounting all this to explain the rage, frustration, and ambivalence of the early queer liberationists about the bars. They were oppressive outgrowths of the closet that encouraged alcoholism and self-hatred, and that made gay people easy targets. After Stonewall, we developed alternative, queer-controlled, community spaces: coffeehouses and restaurants, concerts, dances, and arts festivals. *Gay Community News* itself was founded as a calendar (although it soon developed into an actual weekly newspaper), to inform people about these kinds of activities, and to keep them out of the bars. (This meant, by the way, that we immediately cut off our most likely source of income, bar ads.)

And yet, as much as we criticized the bars, we loved them. They were exciting. They were full of sexual energy and potential romance. For someone like me, marginalized and introverted, the experience of belonging to an exclusive, secret community was even more intoxicating than the beers we were encouraged to drink. I would go to Sporters with my gay male friends on Thursday nights after we had finished laying out that week's edition of *Gay Community News*. I would go to The Saints on Wednesdays and Saturdays. There was always that moment, at the height of the dancing and flirting, when I felt simply ecstatic, in love with everyone there.

That the event that marks the beginning of the modern LGBTQ movement took place at a bar—and a particularly seedy one—is hardly surprising. Many of the queer folk involved in the riot were the most marginalized among us—drag queens, trans women, hustlers, butch dykes, street people, many of them people of color. Bar patrons generally included closeted people from many walks of life, whose livelihoods and families would be utterly wrecked if their arrests were publicized (which they often were, leading to not a few suicides). The raid on the

Stonewall was not the first raid any of them had experienced. It was not the first time they'd faced arrest, beating, public humiliation. The Stonewall riot was not the first time bar patrons had resisted arrest, either, but it was the first time the resistance caught fire. The riot against the police lasted three days, and it drew in people from the neighborhood and around the city. It sparked a movement.

Timing is everything. As queer leader Urvashi Vaid has pointed out, "Stonewall has to be placed within the times and politics of the 1960s—civil rights, Black power, feminist emergence, sexual liberation, rock and roll and drugs and anti-establishment culture on the one hand, and massive white nationalism, state-sponsored assassinations of Black leadership, the murders of two Kennedys in one decade" on the other. The queer groups that organized after Stonewall no longer had secretive, incomprehensible names—Mattachine Society, Daughters of Bilitis—as had those founded in the 1950s. Instead they had names like Gay Liberation Front (GLF). In *Gay Community News*'s Stonewall tenth anniversary issue, Lee Swislow (now former executive director of gay legal advocacy group GLAD; then activist-around-town) wrote about the impact GLF's name had on her: "At some point I heard about Stonewall in New York and about gay people getting together to start the GLF. There were a lot of different liberation fronts then, inspired by Vietnam's National Liberation Front. I pretty much felt I should support anyone who was radical enough to name their group after the NLF." Not to mention, to include the word "gay" in the name. For years, *Gay Community News* was the only listing in the telephone book under "gay"; we fielded calls of every sort, from advice for the lovelorn to suicidal teenagers.

It's significant that Lee writes, "At some point . . ." Like her and most other people in the world, I knew nothing about Stonewall when it was happening. The riot was barely mentioned in the media outside of New York City. And even there, coverage consisted of a few brief articles in the *New York Times*, buried on inside pages (the first headlined "Hostile Crowd Dispersed Near Sheridan Square"—actually, dispersing the crowd took days), and two cover stories in the *Village Voice*. This was not the *Village Voice* of later years, however; the articles' ambivalently homophobic tone might surprise many readers. Still, the *Voice* writers immediately recognized the rebellion as an unprecedented expression of "gay power," a phrase they placed in quotation marks. Because it was new. The writers and editors didn't know what to make of it. Like "liberation front," the phrase was modeled on the slogan of another radical movement, Black Power.

Word of the rebellion spread slowly across the world through queer dish and the occasional newsletter—not through the mainstream media. Indeed, the riot inspired, among many other things, the development of an LGBTQ media to report on our lives, which were covered nowhere else. *Gay Community News* and *Fag Rag* in Boston, *Gay Sunshine* in San Francisco, the Washington, D.C., *Blade*, and many other journals, newspapers, and publishers were founded during the first few years following the Stonewall riots to answer the need of the queer community for sources of news and reflection about itself. (This is not to say that gay and lesbian publications did not exist before Stonewall: most significantly, the monthlies *One*, published by the gay male Mattachine Society, and the *Ladder*, published by the Daughters of Bilitis, were founded in the 1950s and continued publishing through the 1970s. Some cities also had "bar rags," which were basically like shoppers' guides, only with personal listings and bar ads instead of store coupons and community swaps—Boston's was called *Michael's Thing*. And the *Advocate*, which likes to remind readers that it has now been publishing continuously for fifty years, was founded as a biweekly in 1967.)

The Stonewall riots inspired other direct actions. In 1970 Christopher Street Liberation Day was held in New York on the first anniversary of the riots, and soon the practice spread. Boston's first gay pride march was held on Saturday, June 26, 1971. During those early years, organizers insisted that the event was a march, a demonstration —*not* a parade. It had a radical agenda. Boston's History Project writes that the first march "highlight[ed] four oppressive institutions in Boston: the police, the government, hostile bars, and religious institutions." Marchers visited symbols of each: police headquarters, the State House, Jaques bar, and a Catholic church. Only in later decades did the march welcome lesbian and gay police (on whom the police detailed to protect the march would turn their backs); floats sponsored by bars; and contingents from mainline churches (not just the rebel LGBTQ groups). These days Pride parades include not only politicians (who were banned from the early marches in Boston) but also representatives of multinational corporations and banks—something that would have astonished (and likely appalled) the original demonstrators.

I went to my first Lesbian and Gay Pride March in 1978. The previous year, poet and *Fag Rag* editor Charley Shively, the march's keynote speaker, demonstrated his rejection of mainstream institutions by burning a Bible, his Harvard diploma, his University of

Massachusetts teaching contract, and his insurance policies, causing a huge uproar. So I wasn't sure what to expect. I went with my girlfriend, a high school teacher in a Boston suburb, who wore a bag over her head for fear of being recognized by students or parents. At the last minute, her roommate and I persuaded her that she did not also have to wear gloves. She'd become paranoid that she'd be identified by her hands. She was not the only person who marched anonymously.

In the fall of that year, I started working at *Gay Community News* as features editor and was responsible for putting together the June 1979 Stonewall tenth anniversary issue. The anniversary was significant to the queer community but it was nothing like today's public celebration. Along with Lee Swislow's essay, which I mentioned earlier, the issue also included an article by Cindy Rizzo (writing under the pseudonym Cindy Stein) about mainstream press coverage of the riots, such as it was; historical pieces by John D'Emilio and Joe Interrante; a couple of incoherent blurbs by people who said they had worked at the Stonewall; and an article by Karla Jay about organizing New York's first lesbian dance, a controversial and even dangerous project, as the managers of the city's lesbian bars tried to eliminate the competition. We also reprinted Adrienne Rich's essay "The Meaning of Our Love for Women Is What We Constantly Have to Expand" (I was very proud of getting permission to use it).

The issue opened with an unsigned editorial (written by managing editor Richard Burns and me) called "A Stonewall Nation." That term was Richard's. I remember objecting to it, because at the time I saw Stonewall as having relevance mainly for gay men. I thought the participants had been mostly men, and I wasn't sure what lessons the riots had for lesbian feminists like me. So my contribution to the editorial includes acknowledgment of divergent interests among the various groups in the "Stonewall nation," especially between lesbians and gay men, but also between people of different classes and races. It concludes (from Richard) with the hope that a shared queer identity would overcome these divisions. I wasn't so sure about that: the piece uses the word "struggle" a lot—a word I favored at the time.

And, in fact, the movement split almost instantly. Most lesbians left the GLF after a year or so, appalled by their brothers' misogyny, and founded groups such as Radicalesbians and Lesbian Feminist Liberation. They also joined feminist organizations such as NOW—which was not all that happy to have them. Reclaiming an abusive term hurled at them by Betty Friedan, lesbians wearing Lavender Menace T-shirts famously disrupted a NOW meeting and forced the group to recognize their presence and contribution.

The movement also split between queer liberationists like those of New York's Gay Liberation Front and gay rights activists like those of the city's Gay Activists Alliance. Tension between these two tendencies continues to characterize the modern movement: a rights perspective that frames the movement's issues fairly narrowly, as those affecting gay men and lesbians directly, that works on legislative change, and that insists that queer people's needs and aspirations are just like everyone else's; and a liberation perspective, that frames the movement broadly, as interconnected with other movements for social justice, that works on cultural and institutional change, and that elevates the unique contributions and culture of LGBTQ people. These two tendencies are not always mutually exclusive;

liberationists join political campaigns, rights advocates march in demonstrations—and everybody gets married (more on that later).

The meaning of Stonewall has changed since those early years—and will continue to. Its relevance to gay men versus lesbians doesn't feel like an important debate these days, as we've learned more about lesbian participation. We dykes were there, just as we were and are in all movements for social justice. In our current moment, what I and many others find most inspiring about Stonewall is its leadership by gender rebels. Upending the gender binary, along with other sorts of binaries that define humanity in limiting ways—boy/girl; Black/white; Christian/Jew; upper/lower; in/out—leads away from accommodation and toward thoroughgoing, positive social change.

FOR THE FIFTIETH ANNIVERSARY of the Stonewall riot in June 2019, I received all sorts of invitations to speak—on panels, as a keynote. Suddenly I was the 2,000-year-old lesbian. But I was seventeen in 1969, still in high school, not out, not even considering it, just figuring I was a freak. Like most people, I never heard of the Stonewall riots until years later. Even ten years on, and despite editing a special issue about them, I was still not entirely certain whether they constituted the key moment in queer liberation that they have come to signify. Nevertheless, thanks to what I have experienced and written over the decades, it seems I am now an expert.

Strangely, or perhaps not, during all of the celebrations of Stonewall 50, there was little discussion of the most crucial and traumatic event to befall the queer community since the riots: the AIDS epidemic among gay men during the 1980s and '90s. In hindsight, and with regret, I was guilty of this myself in my remarks at various commemorations, even though I had written an entire book (*Hospital Time*, 1997) about the epidemic and what it meant to me and those around me. I spoke about the LGBTQ movement as though it started in 1969 and then sort of jumped into the twenty-first century. But if we want to understand where we are today and how we got here, of course we need to talk about the epidemic. As a community, we lost a generation. As individuals, we lost partners, friends, colleagues, and comrades.

I'm not sure why the Stonewall 50 celebrations so often left out AIDS. Maybe it was all just too painful. Perhaps it was because they were meant to be joyful. Balloons, parties, parades—AIDS does not fit easily into all that. Instead of cute pictures of long-haired men and women smiling, fists raised, it evokes images of young men disfigured by lesions, gasping for breath, emaciated, vomiting, while we who loved and cared for them attended two or more funerals in one day, day after day. We demonstrated too, of course. We had die-ins.

Unlike earlier commemorations of Stonewall—the tenth, and even the twenty-fifth—Stonewall 50 grabbed the attention of the general public, well beyond the queer community. News anchors reported it; magazines ran features; my *parents* knew about it. Were the organizers too young to remember or, aware of their audience, reluctant to dwell on those terrible days? After all, straight people did not acquit themselves particularly well during the crisis (with, of course, exceptions, including Mathilde Krim, founder of the American

Foundation for AIDS Research, and Elizabeth Taylor, who became an outspoken fundraiser). Having AIDS was often seen as a crime: people with HIV/AIDS were accused of spreading their disease to "innocent" citizens and arrested—by police wearing bright yellow protective gloves. Even some health care personnel would not touch people with AIDS—originally called GRID, "gay-related immune deficiency"—if they treated them at all. When I started to visit weekly with a sick friend, *Gay Community News* staffer and AIDS Action Committee founder Bob Andrews, our mutual friend Roberta Stone (now my wife) warned me, "If you have to call an ambulance, don't tell them what he has or they won't come." Some sufferers had to sue dentists and doctors in order to receive care. People with AIDS were evicted from apartments, fired from jobs, ejected from their families, expelled from schools, and ostracized by their communities. Friends and lovers were excluded from family funerals. Never mind, we created our own. At Bob's, his tricks extolled him at an open mic.

A cliché about the AIDS epidemic is that it finally brought gay men and lesbians back together after they parted ways after Stonewall, as lesbians cared for their dying gay brothers. I suppose this is true to some extent, but at least in Boston—where *Gay Community News*, equally women and men (at least aspirationally), shaped much of the organizing—LGBTQ folks had been working together and caring for each other for years. We already knew how to do it. And many of us lesbians had considerable expertise in community-led health initiatives from years of being involved in the women's health movement. We had learned that we could not always trust our doctors and that we had to fight for decent care. When gay men awoke to the horror that the medical system didn't care about them, they drew on our expertise in making trouble, and creating alternative avenues to care.

Perhaps more significantly, though, is the way the AIDS crisis vindicated and reinforced the insights of the liberationist wing of the movement. AIDS simply could not be contained within a narrow "gay" focus. Because AIDS was defined early as a disease of homosexuals, Haitians, and junkies, nobody in the political, medical, or social service establishments felt obligated to do anything about it. We had no choice but to do all of it ourselves—the caregiving, the treatment, the research, the public education. Our organizing, to be effective, had to take on the epidemic from all sides: the racist, homophobic way it was framed; the challenge it posed to the health care system; the indifference of politicians; the scientists who saw people with AIDS as juicy experimental subjects; the religious leaders who saw the disease as divine retribution for sin, a blessing in disguise.

At the same time, as the disease disastrously spread to additional populations, treatments eventually emerged that made the disease chronic and survivable—at least for those who could gain access to and afford them. And it occurs to me that at that point the traumatized LGBTQ movement went into a kind of retreat, focusing more and more narrowly on the single goal of same-sex marriage, which it fought for in statehouses and courts. Many liberationists—myself included—criticized this focus as an accommodationist attempt to join an oppressive institution that had only harmed us. What had happened to the feminist critique of marriage as a foundation of patriarchy? What had the family ever done for queer people except condemn and reject us? Yet, as the movement for same-sex marriage had victories in the courts and legislatures, and finally became the law of the land, things began to look a little different.

For one thing, even some of the most outspoken queer critics of same-sex marriage got married. Myself included. I still want to reject the regulation by the state of our intimate relationships—but marriage afforded protections that we'd never dreamed of. We could keep our kids and be recognized as their parents. We could be covered by our spouse's health insurance. We could inherit a deceased partner's pension and Social Security. We could visit our loved ones in the hospital and demand information from their doctors: I never used the word "wife" so much as when Roberta was hospitalized with a stroke. Some people were welcomed back into their families, sinners no longer. Even marriage turns out to be intersectional, with implications for family, health care, labor, and many other aspects of daily life.

SO HERE WE ARE, "socially isolated" in our homes, if we are lucky enough to have homes and health, masking and washing our hands and our groceries. Worrying. Grieving. My own parents were in their nineties, in an assisted-living apartment, when, as in many institutions for the elderly, COVID-19 began to spread among their neighbors. My father collapsed in early May as his home health aide was helping him to bed. It was the virus. He was hospitalized, seemed to be improving, then died in his sleep. Alone. My family could not gather to mourn him, could not hold the immediate funeral our Jewish tradition prescribes. Instead, we had a shiva on Zoom, attended by nearly a hundred people who wanted to remember his buoyant spirit and his generosity. But it was not like a real shiva. We could not hug, we could not tell stories about him, we could not simply chat about our day and eat cake.

My mother, frail and confused, survives him, and I can visit her if the weather is nice enough for us to sit outside. I can't go up to their apartment to see that my father is no longer in his usual place on their couch. He has slipped out of my life in a way I could never have imagined. And I blame Donald Trump and his vile malevolence and incompetence—he and his spineless toadies, running around like chickens without heads, while squawking daily that everything is fine, great. Perfect! Along with a distressingly substantial proportion of our fellow Americans, they trample and reject the humanity of ever-expanding categories of people—including immigrants, people of color, transfolk, disabled people, Muslims, Jews, and women.

More than ever, the lessons of queer liberation over the past fifty years are crucial. Stonewall demonstrates the power—the necessity—of creative rebellion against oppressive structures and of working together for justice and peace. Without that, we and our planet won't survive. As queer poet W. H. Auden wrote, on the eve of another disaster, in "September 1, 1939":

> There is no such thing as the State
> And no one exists alone;
> Hunger allows no choice
> To the citizen or the police;
> We must love one another or die.

WHAT WOULD HEALTH SECURITY LOOK LIKE?

Sunaura Taylor

IF THERE IS ONE THING this pandemic is making abundantly clear, it is that our health is interconnected: we are joined to each other, to our political and economic systems, to the broader ecology, and to the other species we share the planet with.

The pandemic, after all, has made disturbingly visible that we are all only as healthy as our social support systems. As Anand Giridharadas put it: "Your health is as safe as that of the worst-insured, worst-cared-for person in your society." In the United States, decades of cuts to our nation's social safety net have left us struggling to respond to COVID-19 with an appallingly inadequate public health sector, almost nonexistent job security, and a government more concerned with maintaining profits than saving people's lives.

At the same time, the pandemic reveals that our bodies function more like sponges than fortresses. In a variety of visualizations, we see our bodies extending beyond their usual bounds: graphics of our coughs, sneezes, and even breath show how far beyond our own skin our bodies reach; the six-foot rule of social distancing a daily acknowledgement that our bodies not only leak and ooze, but that they absorb the conditions of others. Our sensitivity to each other's physical presence has never felt more visceral.

And the pandemic exposes connections beyond our species. We know that environmental destruction aided the conditions that led to this outbreak: deforestation, rising temperatures, and the loss of habitat all forced species into closer contact with each other, including with our own. It is increasingly clear that this virus, just like the many other zoonotic viruses that have come before, jumped from one species to another (in this case, likely from bats or pangolins), aided by the consumption of wild animals and the global increase in unsanitary and brutal factory farms.

The spread of the virus from humans to cats, dogs, and even the Bronx Zoo's tigers has brought us crashing back into the animal world, reminding us that our bodies are enmeshed with the bodies of other creatures and ecosystems. To this point, Giridharadas might have added that your health is only as safe as the most endangered species, the most exploited industrialized food animal. Or, that of the most clear-cut forest, the worst-regulated and polluted ecosystem.

THE IDEA THAT OUR HEALTH is connected to and interdependent with the health of other people, environments, and social structures is of course not new. Indeed, a brief look at the shared roots of public health and environmental protection exposes that such connections helped shape the mandates of government agencies for over a century.

While it could be argued that the origins of both the public health and environmental movements date as far back as the earliest drainage systems, toilets, and water systems in ancient history, the sanitary movement and the social reformers of the nineteenth century deserve an abundance of credit for birthing environmental concern in this country. These reformers recognized the role of dirty water, smog-filled air, piling waste, and inadequate housing as serious threats to human health and well-being—particularly among the urban poor.

The first U.S. boards of health were established after epidemics of cholera and yellow fever broke out in the late eighteenth century. Such diseases were claiming thousands of lives, with outbreaks often occurring in areas with dirty water and unsanitary conditions. As with the COVID-19 pandemic, people most vulnerable to infectious disease already endured poverty, environmental contamination, structural racism, and inadequate health care as preexisting conditions. Throughout the nineteenth century, the poor were largely blamed for diseases that decimated their communities, but social reformers identified poverty, overcrowding, unhygienic housing, and inadequate waste disposal as the cause; they advocated for the construction of safe water supplies, sewage systems, and street cleaning. Early boards of health became models for local and state public health agencies, which among other things became responsible for controlling disease through sanitation, air pollution control, and clean water supplies.

At this time environmental health, public health, and occupational health were largely understood as a single discipline, which emphasized disease prevention and social reform and which focused on the living and working conditions of people in urban communities. By the beginning of the twentieth century, however, the field began to separate into the three distinct arenas we know today, all of which were increasingly informed by advances in science and technology. Still, these disciplines were connected enough that, by the 1930s, labor movements advocating for what historian Jennifer Klein identifies as "health security" in the New Deal era would often include dimensions of all three. Tracing the history of the labor movement's early struggles for a more expansive welfare state, Klein writes, in her book *For All These Rights* (2003), that "the politics of the New Deal put security at the center of American political and economic life." "Labor," she explains, "saw health security as part of a broad economic security project," with policy proposals that included "occupational safety, industrial health, and public health demands."

Klein details how labor's multifaceted visions of health security were thwarted by the emergence of such incentives as employee benefits programs, including employer-based health insurance, a much more limited effort. U.S. industry aggressively fought to reduce the links between workers and the state by offering benefits tied to employment. After World War II, Klein writes, "American business firms and commercial insurance companies became partners in creating and expanding nonstate alternatives to public social insurance." As well as detailing the history that has left workers in the United States at the mercy of this employment-dependent system, Klein's project also exposes that there once was a far broader vision of what health care could look like, and it included environmental public health.

"The health security movement's emphasis on community-based models could have changed the American conception of health care in significant ways," Klein writes. "Less focused on technology intensive hospital care, they might have allocated resources and attention more equally between clinical medical services and policies addressing the economic and environmental factors that affect health." As COVID-19 lays bare not only the inadequacies of employee-based health insurance and the U.S. social safety net, but the economic and environmental impacts on health as well, the urgency of reclaiming this more expansive vision of health security is undeniable.

AS ENVIRONMENTAL PROTECTION drifted away from its roots in public health and social reform, and as organized labor's expansive visions for health care faded, the economic growth of the postwar United States increasingly took a terrible environmental toll. As the effects of industrial pollution became visible in smog-filled skies, contaminated rivers, and shrinking wild spaces, a growing percentage of the public became concerned with environmental protection, sparking the environmental movement of the 1960s and '70s.

Yet, despite the clear public health implications of the growing environmental crises, the burgeoning environmental groups of the time traced their origins not to the health reformers and "sanitary science" champions of the industrial era, many of whom were women, but to the conservation movement of the nineteenth century—a movement, as a myriad of environmental historians have pointed out, shaped by eugenicist, masculinist, and white supremacist ideas. This genealogy had the unfortunate effect of shaping a U.S. environmental movement that for decades focused more on protecting pristine wilderness, largely for white leisure, than on protecting polluted urban environments and the communities of color living in them.

Responding to pressure from the movement, Nixon created the Environmental Protection Agency (EPA) in 1970, severing public health authority from environmental protection at the policy level. Federal and state health departments had historically housed responsibility for many of the nation's environmental programs, including the protection of water and air. Those same agencies dealt with preventive health services, maternal and child health, nursing, health records, statistics, and local health administration. The Nixon administration removed environmental responsibility from these departments, consolidating them into a new agency, in order to put forward a more efficient and comprehensive environmental program.

The creation of the EPA was largely met with excitement; health departments, after all, had often failed miserably to protect the environment, a challenging task given the dearth of environmental regulations at the time. The new structure brought much needed funding and attention to environmental issues. Yet the separation of environmental agencies from public health also led to a steady decline in the role of public health perspectives within them. While a fundamental mission of the EPA to this day is to protect public health, such approaches and leadership have largely been neglected. The Institute of Medicine's 1988 report *The Future of Public Health* lamented, "The removal of public health authority from environmental agencies has led to fragmented responsibility, lack of coordination, and inadequate attention to the public health dimensions of environmental issues."

This cleaved human from nonhuman health in matters of public policy, only a few years before environmental justice and environmental health movements began advocating for the idea that the two can not be productively separated. In the late 1970s, people whose communities had experienced the severe health impacts from toxic water and air pollution began identifying and challenging the ways environmental harm is distributed along racial and class lines. Ever since then, these movements have asserted that health and racial justice are at the heart of environmental protection, and that the health of people and environments are entangled.

The split between environmental protection and public health has also institutionalized the idea that human bodies and communities are separate from "nature"—that people are impermeable, independent, self-sustaining, and individually bounded entities that can be protected with the right health insurance package. This narrow technocratic structure diminishes understandings of how health and vulnerability to injury are things that cross both species and environmental boundaries and are fundamentally entangled.

THE PANDEMIC IS MAKING these entanglements visible, exposing not only our connections—to each other, to other species, to our environments—but also the vectors of connection through bodily vulnerability to illness, dependency, injury, and disability. In previous work, I have called this network of connections "disabled ecologies," the trails of disability that are created—spatially, temporally, and across species boundaries—when ecosystems are contaminated, depleted, and profoundly altered. While disabled ecologies are all around us—emerging from the climate crisis, from contaminated Superfund sites, from deforestation and fossil fuel extraction—the pandemic's disabled ecology is forcing a response from a global system that has thus far failed to act on environmental catastrophe.

Yet the response to this pandemic in the United States has often denied our connections and interdependence. From the beginning we have been told with relief that the virus is mostly dangerous for the elderly and those with preexisting conditions—as if these people are not us and the ones we love. The conditions that make someone more vulnerable to COVID-19 are of course intimately tied up with poverty, environmental racism, and inadequate health care. Thus while such a sentiment is unabashedly ableist—should we mourn the lives of the healthy and robust more than the lives of the ill and disabled?—it is also deeply racialized, a message to the white middle class that they have no need to panic. In addition, we have been alerted to the real possibility that overburdened hospitals with limited medical supplies might withhold treatment from disabled patients with COVID-19. Already disability rights organizations have filed various lawsuits against such rationing guidelines in several states.

The truth is that over 60 percent of the population in the United States has a chronic health condition, and 40 percent has more than one. A disproportionate number of disabled individuals are poor and working-class people of color, employed as "essential workers," a euphemism that covers up the devastating reality that the majority has no safety net, no health insurance, and no PPE. Essential, and yet dying in vast numbers. Calls for the country to reopen, and for vulnerable people to continue to isolate, only serve to center visions of able, healthy, and independent individuals in a pristine world as the norm, even as the climate crisis and rising global inequity make an increasing majority of us—and the ecosystems we live in—sick and impaired. The human and nonhuman beings who are ill and disabled continue to be represented as elsewhere. But they are not marginal. They are us.

Meanwhile, the current administration has given a green light to polluters, lifting emissions regulations long set by federal environmental laws. It has offered bailouts to fossil fuel and meat industries, the very industries most responsible for the environmental crises we are facing.

While various news stories have pointed to the decrease in air pollution during the pandemic, evidence suggests that communities living in areas with high industrial pollution are more likely to have higher rates of COVID-19 cases. And because emissions regulations are not currently being enforced, industries may be more emboldened than ever to pour toxins into these same areas. The predominantly Black communities of Louisiana's "Cancer Ally," for example, have some of the highest death rates of COVID-19 in the country. As a recent piece on VICE put it, "The risk factor list for severe coronavirus cases issued by the CDC is a litany of conditions aggravated or caused by pollution: asthma, chronic obstructive pulmonary disease (COPD), heart disease, hypertension, and diabetes." For communities long on the frontlines of environmental racism, ecological and human harm rise together.

In January 2016, following the popularity of the new slogan "The Future Is Female," Alice Wong's website, the Disability Visibility Project, announced the creation of the hashtag #thefutureisdisabled. On the day the hashtag was announced, Wong wrote: "You might wonder, 'What the hell is The Future Is Disabled?' Does it sound ominous? Hopeful? Inevitable? What does it mean?" While the trending hashtag was meant as a way of challenging eugenicist legacies—a way of claiming the future for disabled people and disabled perspectives (indeed, another variation of the appropriated slogan was #thefutureisaccessible)—I always thought of the slogan through an ecological frame, as a way of conceptualizing climate breakdown, mass extinction, and mutation. Since COVID-19 has hit the world, it seems to me that the future has arrived far sooner than expected.

FOR DECADES disabled communities have taught us that, while injury and sickness are fundamental to life, our response to injury and sickness is a societal issue. At this moment—as the vulnerability and dependency of our bodies is so undeniably entangled with the health of ecosystems and other species—it is time to recognize ourselves as an increasingly disabled people in increasingly disabled landscapes. How then should we respond to injury?

Perhaps, to start, we can rethink the separation of human health from the health of our environments and social welfare systems. What has been lost by breaking off environmental protection from public health agencies and by narrowing an expansive vision of health security to a fight for access to health care?

Hope for a radical expansion of, and marriage between, environmental remediation and health security might seem naive, given our deeply engrained for-profit health care system and the dismal funding history of the EPA. But today's extraordinary crises—rising global authoritarianism, spectacular levels of inequality, increasing deregularization, environmental devastation, and a global pandemic—have increased calls for a just response. And activists have already modeled such a vision. Movements for environmental justice, climate justice, indigenous sovereignty, disability justice, as well as new public health frames—such as the growing concept of "One Health" and recent calls for a New Deal for Public Health—are championing the idea that the health of humans is inseparable from the health of the environment. Indeed, a myriad of scientists, medical professionals, activists, and government agencies are telling us that we are facing a global health crisis because the health of our environments is in extreme peril. The COVID-19 pandemic makes clear that struggles for Medicare for All and a Green New Deal are two sides of the same coin. We urgently need them both—and more.

But we also need to rethink our relationship to disability and illness as a society. The future is disabled, but that need not be foreboding. It could signal a future that recognizes and supports our mutual vulnerability as creatures on this planet, a future that is structured around our interdependence with each other and the environments and species we live with, and a future that pursues access for people at all stages of life and abilities. Even if we could miraculously stop the spread of COVID-19 and the climate crisis tomorrow, we will be treating the injury to our altered ecosystems and the beings who live with them for years to come. The future is indeed disabled, but what we do in the present will define whether that future can be hopeful.

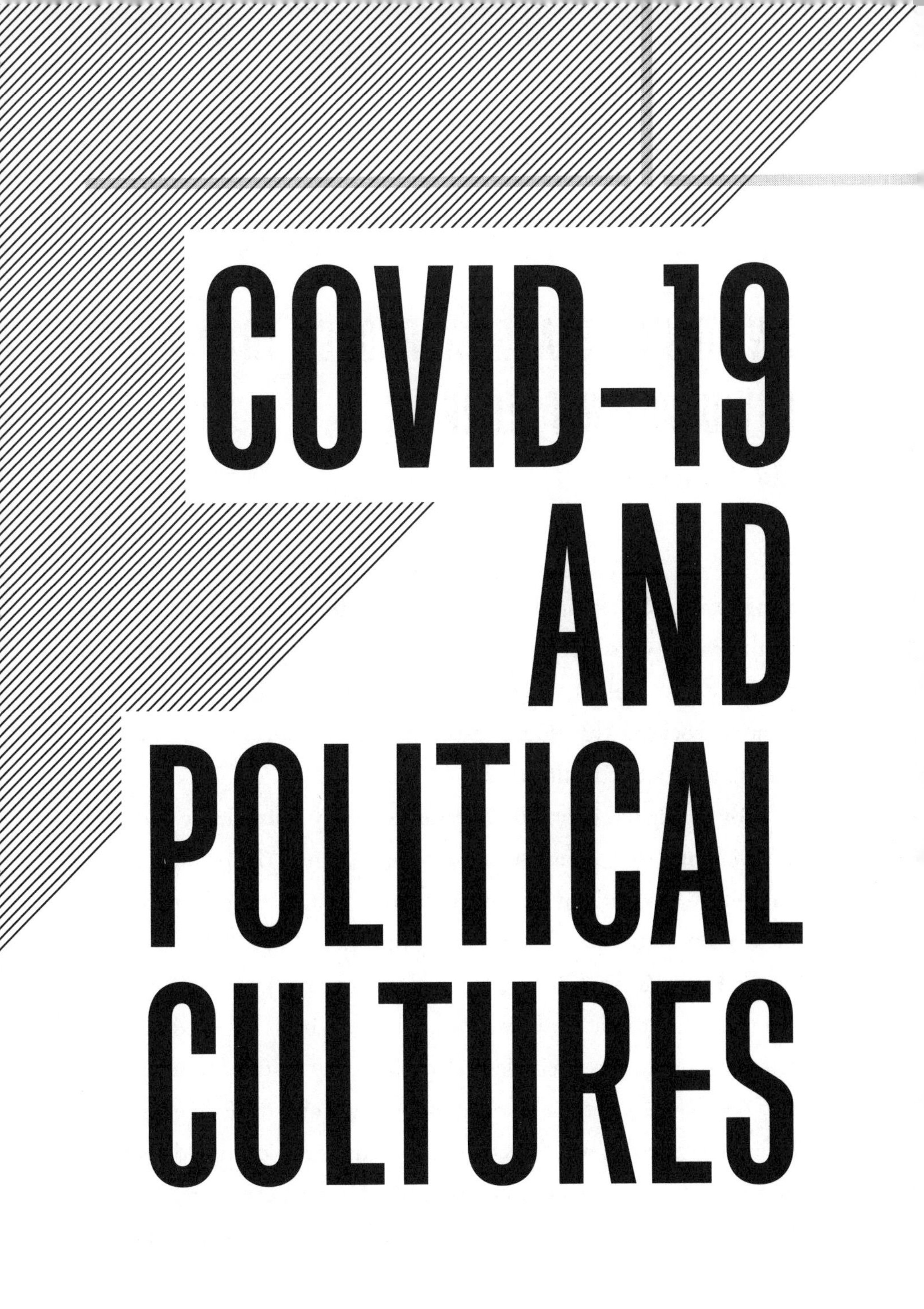

COVID-19 AND POLITICAL CULTURES

SWEDEN'S RELAXED APPROACH TO COVID-19 ISN'T WORKING

Adele Lebano

AS AN ITALIAN living in Sweden, I am accustomed to being surprised by the many ways that Sweden is different—not just from Italy, but from its own reputation as an exceptionally virtuous country and a model society. This double estrangement is especially dismaying during this public health crisis.

By letting its citizens live their lives mostly as usual, the Swedish government's soft, noninterventionist approach to the pandemic has challenged the paths undertaken by other countries and the recommendations of the World Health Organization (WHO). Sweden has decided to go *lagom*—a Swedish word that means "just right," neither too much nor too little. Few restrictions have been imposed; people are mostly asked to keep clean and physically distant. Sweden has also decided not to track the disease's spread, and its testing lags far behind other countries. This may be a realistic choice in anticipation of a lockdown that would be unsustainable for people and for the economy, but it still feels odd. The "right" response to the pandemic has been elusive, but different local approaches do say something about our conceptions of politics and society—about our ideas of life and attachments and the links between private values and public choices.

Despite the disagreement among analysts and foreign media on its appropriateness, both explain Sweden's soft way of managing COVID-19 as a reflection of Nordic individualism, as well as trust in institutions and in fellow citizens. People will do the right thing out of a sense of responsibility, it is thought. They do not need to be coerced into a lockdown because they can be trusted to act properly. Yet crowded streets and bustling play parks may tell a different story.

In Sweden these days, high schools are closed, and university classes have moved online, but university canteens are open. People are encouraged to work from home, and a ban on meetings of 500 people, later reduced to 50, was introduced in March and extended until December. Yet elementary schools, where social distance is hard to observe and certainly more than 50 gather, remain open and compulsory. There are no restrictions on supermarkets, shopping malls, indoor amusement parks, or public transit. I see no change when looking at crowded restaurants and cafés, or at holiday celebrations. Young people seem to hug and kiss more than usual. The warmth and light of spring and summer make people here come back to life after the long winter. My neighbors in the countryside invited three different families to stay over for Easter weekend, and they all happily shared the house and meals.

April 30 is when Valborg celebrations take place all over Sweden. In Uppsala, where I live, alumni of all ages usually convene at 3 p.m. outside the university's main library to welcome spring. There are bonfires and celebrations. This year the events were all canceled due to COVID-19. But walking through town, I heard loud music reverberating from students' buildings, which made me think the parties had just moved inside. The minister of the interior, while speaking in defense of the Swedish way of fighting the pandemic, threatened harder measures should the population not respect recommendations for social distancing. Meanwhile, in Lund, another university town, the municipality dumped manure in public parks to discourage gatherings.

Still, as of early August, the total confirmed COVID-19 deaths in Sweden has passed 5,700, a relatively small number when compared to Italy, the United Kingdom, or the United States, but much worse than neighbors Denmark (616), Norway (256), and Finland (329), which all elected to lock down. Sweden's 572 COVID-19 deaths per million people compares poorly to theirs, as well: Denmark (111); Norway (48); Finland (61).

Despite this, Sweden's public health authorities have not fundamentally changed their approach. With regard to schools, for example, Sweden's Public Health Agency states, "as long as siblings or other members of the family do not show symptoms of disease they can go to school, preschool, or their workplace." Parents, like me, who would rather keep their kids home are constantly reminded that school is compulsory in Sweden. In many cases—and at odds with Sweden's soft approach to the public health emergency—parents are warned that they will be reported to social services for keeping their children out of school. Meanwhile, schools admit that they can do little to protect kids from the virus, beyond showing them how to wash their hands properly and use hand sanitizer.

The government's mild and contradictory measures largely rest on the view of state epidemiologist Anders Tegnell, who believes that the soft approach will help the country cope in the long run because the virus is here to stay, and sooner or later most people will probably get it. Swedish media and even a former prime minister, Carl Bildt, have expressed confidence that Swedish character—a combination of trust in institutions, loose family ties, and an inclination to social distancing—will see the country through the pandemic.

Some have voiced concerns over the lack of protective equipment for health care workers. Others say the relaxed measures have resulted in too many deaths. In an editorial in the *Dagens Nyheter*, a major Swedish newspaper, a group of scientists from the Karolinska Institute, Uppsala University, and Chalmers University of Technology called the architects of the strategy "officials without the talents to predict or control the epidemic," and urged the government to intervene with "radical measures." But such dissonant voices and sporadic organized resistance—for example, among teachers—have been rare. For the most part, the Swedes back up the government and its choices.

Is the proclaimed belief in the Swedish character and individual responsibility at the heart of the country's response to COVID-19? What I have witnessed seems instead to bear the mark of an organicist society, one in which individual freedom always gives way to public good, where individuals' goals and expectations are shaped by the will of the government. Indeed, the secret to Sweden's exceptionalism rests in a social compact that limits—not expands—people's reliance on each other because it fosters dependence on the state. The Swedish formula, I think, combines anomie—lack of social and moral norms, not individualism in the liberal sense—with organicism.

In Sweden government action against COVID-19 has been relaxed and contradictory, and so have people's responses. At the root of the synergy is a unique pact between state and citizens. The state provides for people's material needs so that they will not have to depend on each other for their welfare nor be exposed to chance. In exchange, citizens trust the state to make decisions in their interest. Trust, or the confidence that a party will act fairly and in the interest of the other party, is an essential element of society. When there is trust, people do not need to act defensively or attack out of fear of being attacked. In the absence of complete information, trust supports stability and reduces uncertainty.

Yet trust maintains an element of conditionality. Trust is gained, but it is also tested and revoked if not honored. For trust in government to be a good thing, citizens need to keep doubting, examining, questioning, and judging governments and their choices. In an organicist society, however, tests on trust cease. And, with blind trust in the government, people are relieved from the responsibility for what happens to their fellow citizens, to their families, and even to themselves. For over a century, the Swedish state has committed to taking care of children, the sick, and the elderly. Yet the bargain is dangerous for its citizens because taking responsibility, listening to one's own needs, and taking care of others is what makes us human and protects us from arbitrary power.

Lebano

A 2006 best-selling book in Sweden, *Är svensken människa? Gemenskap och oberoende i det moderna Sverigea* (Is the Swede Human? Community and Independence in Modern Sweden), makes a similar argument. Its authors, Henrik Berggren and Lars Trägårdh, both challenge and reinforce some stereotypes about Swedish people. They describe the contract between individuals and the state as fostering a form of both radical individualism and total dependence. They call it "the Swedish theory of love."

In contrast to the Millian idea that democracy flourishes where individuals can choose their life commitments and exercise independent critical judgment over institutions and policies, Sweden offers a model of democratic success that favors stability over freedom, dependence on the state over interdependence among citizens. Swedish society, to quote a key Swedish idea, is *folkhemmet*, the "people's home"—a place where, just like in a family, all members have their place and their needs taken care of.

What has struck me as an outsider in Sweden is people's *privateness*, which is not the same as individuality. In the Swedish homes that I visit, life is organized around social rituals and habits that leave little to individual initiatives. Such rituals, I have noticed, defeat socioeconomic differences or political and geographical divides, and in some sense do make Swedes equal. From the décor of the kitchen and living room, to food, to how to celebrate Easter or when to allow kids to eat sweets, the Swedes I have met tend to reflect the Swedish way.

The key ideas of Nordic social democracy are linked with the Lutheran tradition and its strict, unmediated relationship between the individual and God. Full commitment to that relationship leads to salvation. Similarly, an unchallenged, exclusive relationship between the individual and the state is regarded as the path to well-being. Denmark and Norway share the same Lutheran roots; however, they have made a very different choice in the face of the pandemic, enforcing a preventative lockdown to control the spread of the virus. So the source of Sweden's distinctive way is hard to place. Perhaps the quasi-religious allegiance to the state was facilitated by the Socialdemokratiska Arbetareparti's (SAP) long hold on the country. The Swedish version of social democracy was indeed inaugurated by the SAP in the 1930s, and the party has largely dominated the country's political life ever since.

Swedes trust the government and its choices to be "just right." And here the notion of *lagom* appears less humble than one may expect. If the social compact promises that decision-making processes will produce "just right" outcomes, governments don't need good arguments to justify their actions. And if the Swedish approach to COVID-19 is at odds with scientific evidence, it needs little justification, only citizens' trust.

By accepting the compact, citizens agree to embrace the majority view and stand behind government decisions. And the state, committing to take care of its citizens, releases them from the burden of moral choices. Yet even Jean-Jacques Rousseau, considered by some to be the founder of an organicist view of politics, believed that only the never-ending effort to balance individual interests and the public good could produce a "general will." Sweden, by contrast, appears to have "solved" this tension, together with other daunting questions about values, as if basic, competing political ideas such as equality, freedom, and justice have been permanently settled. Welfare protection, material comfort, and social cohesion are obtained by putting aside conflicts of values and moral dilemmas to focus on managerial tasks. Sweden seems to have succeeded in the shift that so concerned Max Weber: turning politics into the management of means.

The Swedish organicist model of democracy encourages citizens to suspend their capacity to choose. And if practice makes perfect, individual agency and moral literacy—as well as untold numbers of lives—are at risk.

LUCKY TO LIVE IN BERLIN

Paul Hockenos

DURING THE LETHAL COVID-19 pandemic, I feel fortunate to live in Germany. Its safety net, reinforced with billions of euros in new state funding, has thus far protected my small family and most of my acquaintances, many of whom, like me, are self-employed. Indeed, when called upon in crisis, the German *Sozialstaat*, or welfare state—even in its present hobbled version—has come to the aid of most of Germany's inhabitants.

Here in Berlin, the virus itself has not hit nearly as hard as in other Western European cities: 221 deaths and 8,802 infections as of July 22. Across Germany, the deaths per 100,000 inhabitants has been one of the lowest in the developed world, about 11 (and half that in Berlin). By comparison, the UK stands at 68, Chile at 45, and the United States at 42. Concentrated, localized outbreaks are still happening, such as earlier this month in central Germany at the industrial meat-processing plant Tönnies, where 1,500 workers—mainly Eastern Europeans sharing cramped quarters—tested positive.

Germany's low toll reflects its early widespread testing, efficient tracking system, as well as prodigious state-of-the-art facilities. Before the crisis, in 2012, Germany had the highest number of ICU beds in Europe, 29 per 100,000 people, compared to 12 in Italy and 6 in the Netherlands. And when the message from the WHO to "test, test, test" came on March 16, Germany immediately began expanding its laboratory facilities for en masse testing. In August, Germany introduced compulsory COVID-19 testing for vacationers returning from high-risk destinations such as Spain.

Very early on, by the end of March, Germany had carried out around 920,000 tests—more than any other European country. The thorough tracking of infections—carried out by otherwise idle college students—meant that many people who had no symptoms were tested simply because they had had contact with someone who had tested positive. In countless cases, the rigorous tracing of infection chains nipped COVID-19's spread in the bud. In contrast, in Italy, Spain, and the United States, testing focused mostly on seriously ill patients at first. This might, in part, explain why so few in Germany have died: the early testing enabled infected people to be treated early.

In Germany, people adhered fairly conscientiously to new laws and state rules governing behavior, which varied within the country by region. While the *New York Times* attributed this to high trust in the state, others suggested it had something to do with the national character: 97 percent of Germans believe scientists' pronouncements on the climate crisis, for example, so were perhaps also inclined to believe the pronouncements of medical professionals. In Berlin, the social distancing regimen has been respected but in a way more relaxed than elsewhere: people could still enjoy parks even at the peak of infections in April, though only in pairs or family groups. At the time, the city was quieter than I have ever known it—bars, clubs, galleries, movie theaters, and restaurants were closed, and traffic reduced. It evoked East Berlin under socialism (time was abundant, no one was in a hurry, most folks went to bed early). Since culture and nightlife are so much of what defines Berlin today, the quietude is still onerous if you're a denizen of the club scene. I'm not, but I'm craving a loud gig in one of my favorite haunts. God knows whether they'll still be there when groups can meet again in such close quarters.

Berlin is known for its small companies, gig economy, and ranks of freelancers, and the economy's overnight shutdown cast millions of people and firms into peril. For many, work evaporated overnight. For example, my friend Colin, a professional translator, told me that overnight the emails from clients simply stopped. A version of this is still being experienced by just about all of Berlin's musicians, writers, filmmakers, photographers, actors—and virtually the entire coterie of Berlin's creative class, much of which just scrapes by at the best of times.

Fortunately, in April more than $1.4 billion was doled out in Berlin to more than 150,000 of the city's self-employed and small businesses. Colin filled out a short online application for the $5,400 that is being offered, no strings attached, to freelancers. To his shock—as Germany's bureaucracy is notoriously ponderous and time-sapping—the sum popped up in his bank account two days later. I did the same and received the payment within days too. Businesses with up to 10 employees have been eligible for up to $15,000—a less helpful injection—but can also receive zero-interest loans, backed by the state.

I don't know of anywhere else in Europe, or for that matter the world, where such a generous and speedy injection went to the smallest cogs of the economy. This speaks to more than just German administrative agility and an economy that has boomed for over a decade, although those surely helped. It is also that Germany's Sozialstaat, the target of so much leftist vitriol in recent years, has lived up to its postwar reputation, despite severe blows in recent decades. While economic disparity has never been wider in the Federal Republic than it is now, the framework of the safety net nonetheless prepared Germany for this crisis.

"The Sozialstaat has been able to help so many people because it could rely on structures that were already there," Joachim Rock of Paritätische Wohlfahrtsverband, a nondenominational charity based in Berlin, told me. "Just about everybody is insured and almost all retirees have pensions. As much as the social welfare state has been pared down, its offices and laws are still there. Additional state monies could flow into them."

The extent to which the injection—with more to come—will tide us over depends on the length of the crisis and the economic turbulence that follows. For someone like Colin, the $5,400 padded his budget for about two months, after he cut expenses to bare bones (Berlin's rents have soared in past years, but it's still possible for artists and others to get by on very little). Without doubt, many small shops and one-shot startups won't make it, which will diminish Berlin's urban landscape indefinitely, and maybe even, in the worst-case scenario, kill off its cool entirely.

Künstlersozialkasse (KSK, Social Insurance for Artists), a state institution that provides support for artists, offers hope as well. The

KSK provides a broad range of creatives, including writers such as myself, with affordable health insurance, long-term care, and pension plans. The logic that brought KSK to life was not benevolence: it was better to have creatives paying at least something into the system, ran the argument, than nothing and then finding them on the streets or the hospitals' steps come old age. Income determines how much one pays to KSK, and that amount is then matched by the state—just as private sector companies match the contributions of their employees. KSK cuts the cost of health insurance in half and doubles social security contributions. When COVID-19 hit, KSK announced that its members could decrease their payments to match their reduced incomes. In the same vein, an April 1 law banned landlords from expelling tenants who couldn't make rent on account of the pandemic.

As for those tossed out of jobs and in need of full welfare services and unemployment, the process to qualify for benefits has been streamlined. Sweeping changes to the Sozialstaat under the 1998–2005 Social Democratic government of Chancellor Gerhard Schröder trimmed welfare benefits and made the criteria for obtaining them more rigorous. Today, however, and presumably for the short term, the unemployed no longer need to prove that their assets are nearly zero in order to receive aid. Local administrations are instructed to focus on getting aid to applicants as fast as possible rather than holding them to the letter of the law.

The first federal €1.25 trillion crisis aid package (three times the entire 2020 budget) throws a lifeline to much larger companies and their workers. At its heart are zero-interest loans as well as

Kurzarbeit, or short-term layoffs, which is a government program that pays workers 60 percent of their wages (or 67 percent, if they have children) when, because of crisis-related shortfalls, a firm must either temporarily lay them off or reduce their hours.

My neighbor owns an advertising firm with thirty full-time employees. When clients started canceling contracts in mid-March, and it became clear that in-person staff meetings were no longer possible, his company continued to pay staff in full. The state will reimburse the firm 60 percent for the hours staff couldn't work because of lost contracts or the need to provide childcare, since day cares and schools also closed. The firm is picking up the remaining 40 percent of the paycheck for those lost hours. Thus all of the employees will receive full payment for at least the next few months.

This scheme is nothing new in Germany. It provides firms with a lifeline when they need it, and it worked commendably during the financial crisis. The difference today is the extraordinary volume: about 4 million people are currently on short-term layoff. My neighbor believes it will help him retain valuable professionals rather than lose them to the market; when business picks up again, his staff will move seamlessly back into their old jobs. And it keeps millions of workers from rushing to the unemployment office, as they have had to do in the United States. In Germany, economists project an estimated 2.5 million people will become unemployed as a result of the crisis; in the United States, 17 million filed for unemployment benefits in the span of three weeks (the ratio of the two countries' populations is roughly 1:4). Experts say that the Kurzarbeit option is limiting economic fallout by 45 percent. But their greatest advantage, they argue, is still to come, as it will speed the private sector's return to normal once the crisis subsides.

As impressive as it is, Germany's short-term layoff scheme is eclipsed by those of other European countries: Denmark and Norway pay the entirety of the furloughed employees' salaries. Austria and the Netherlands chip in 80 to 90 percent. Nevertheless, the emergency measures are extremely popular in Germany, reflected in Merkel's current ratings—the highest in years—and could bolster the social welfare state after the crisis. "There's overwhelming approval for the immediate crisis measures," economist Achim Truger told the weekly *Freitag*. "These are far reaching, and were set into motion quickly and were large in volume. So a lot has happened that would not have been possible in other economic situations." He imagines that some of the measures could remain in place long after the medical crisis.

Rock, of Paritätische Wohlfahrtsverband, argues that while freelance professionals such as me have been administered to admirably, many of the most needy in Germany are falling through the cracks. Welfare payments are so low that simply having children at home for lunch or paying higher prices at the grocery store can stress household budgets to the breaking point. "Most of the soup kitchens and public cafeterias are closed," he says. Associations of welfare recipients have come together to petition for an extra $110 a month to meet these needs—though to no avail, yet.

"The problem is that 60 percent of a small paycheck is very little," Stefan Reinecke of the left-liberal daily *Tageszeitung* told me, referring to the short-term layoff scheme. The vast low-income sector created during the Schröder era struggles to get by even with full pay; many simply can't make it on 60 percent of their usual pay.

Reinecke also notes that while Germany's social solidarity at home has been outstanding, that compassion stops at the border. "It doesn't work internationally," he says, and only in limited fashion across the EU. "This is very shortsighted. This is a different kind of crisis than the euro crisis," says Reinecke. "Europe's hardest-hit countries aren't in such straits because of their economic policies but because of a pandemic. Germany should do a lot more to help them."

Germany's diligence seems to be paying off: in August, schools starts again in Berlin—all pupils at all levels will assemble as usual and resume their studies. We parents pray it lasts.

THE SOLIDARITY ECONOMY

Paul R. Katz & Leandro Ferreira

WHILE BRAZILIAN PRESIDENT Jair Bolsonaro denies that a serious public health crisis is underway, a small municipality an hour up the coast from Rio de Janeiro has instituted a remarkable and effective COVID-19 response. In Maricá, a city of 160,000, about 42,000 of the city's lowest-income residents—who already receive 130 reals (R$), about $25, per month as part of the city's expanded basic income—are now being paid R$300 per month ($60), 169 percent of the Brazilian poverty line, at least through September. As the pandemic took hold, end-of-year bonuses were advanced to make April's payment an even larger R$430 per person. Food baskets are also distributed each month to families with children in the public school system. More than 21,000 self-employed and informal-sector workers with low and moderate incomes are receiving R$1,045 each month, the Brazilian minimum salary, and further direct support is being offered to help small businesses keep workers on their payrolls in the absence of federal action. While the public health impacts of these policies are difficult to assess, other benefits are already clear. Between January and May, the city lost only 0.4 percent of its formal-sector jobs, while the state of Rio lost 5 percent. Meanwhile tax receipts increased in Maricá, in contrast to the sharp declines expected across the country. Numbers like these represent the difference between catastrophe and a level of stability required to overcome the crisis for tens of thousands of Maricá's residents.

This set of initiatives represents the most ambitious city-level response to COVID-19 in Brazil, and one of the most notable in the world. That all of this is happening in a small suburban city on the outskirts of Rio might be surprising to those unfamiliar with the recent political history of the region. To observers of the self-designated City of Utopias, however, there is nothing unusual about the speed or scope of Maricá's COVID-19 response. The sole municipality in the state of Rio de Janeiro governed by the left-leaning Workers' Party (Partido dos Trabalhadores, or PT), for the last decade Maricá has benefitted remarkably from a stroke of geological fortune: its location next to the Campo de Lula, the most productive oil drilling site in Brazil.

Yet unlike the protagonists of countless prior commodity booms, the city has used its windfall to distinguish itself as Brazil's premier municipal innovator, investing its oil proceeds in a remarkable suite of progressive social policies. In addition to the basic income program, which has more than 42,000 monthly recipients, initiatives include savings accounts for high school students, free public transportation, massive infrastructure investments, and a sovereign wealth fund to lower costs of capital and guarantee social programs in perpetuity.

At the center of these policies is a local digital currency called the mumbuca. Most social benefits in Maricá are paid in mumbucas, as are city salaries. The currency is backed one-to-one by reals held in reserve by the Banco Mumbuca, the largest community bank in Brazil, which is funded through the Maricá city budget. The currency is accepted exclusively and almost universally in Maricá. The 2 percent fees that businesses pay to accept the mumbuca, and thus to access its massive base of beneficiaries, go straight to the bank, where they are used to fund no-interest loans for local entrepreneurs and homeowners. The mumbuca, in other words, is not only a vehicle for financial inclusion, but also a means to turn Maricá from a sleepy bedroom community into a thriving market for goods, jobs, and leisure.

The transformation underway in Maricá is rooted in two Brazilian policy visions that have been refined over the past half century: universal basic income and the solidarity economy. Brazil has been, since 2004, the only country in the world to legislate every citizen's right to a basic income. While financial constraints have limited the law's application to the country's neediest citizens, the first step toward its realization, a widely heralded conditional cash transfer program called Bolsa Família, has helped tens of millions to escape poverty. The latter pillar, the "solidarity economy," has been developed in the form of local cooperativism and the world's largest network of state-regulated community banks.

This history helps to explain why, even as Bolsonaro encourages Brazilians to ignore the social distancing guidelines of state and municipal authorities, basic income advocates have managed to push a package through Congress offering R$600 per month to unemployed and informal-sector workers and R$1,200 to single mothers at least through August, and to put a permanent basic income at the center of Brazilian political debate. And it allows us to see Maricá as an object lesson in the power of permanent policy structures to offer rapid emergency responses that favor mutual aid over the rapaciousness that so many peer cities around the world are struggling to hold at bay.

PROPOSALS FOR BASIC INCOME in Brazil began to cohere in the 1970s, a time when policy experts were seeking to reinvigorate struggling welfare states in many parts of the world. Experiments with negative income taxes in the United States and the Mincome initiative in Manitoba seemed to point toward fairer ways to distribute national income. According to Fernando Freitas, whose masters thesis on the history of basic income in Brazil remains the best source on the topic, economist Antonio Maria da Silveira made the country's first formal proposal in 1975, at the tail end of the first "Brazilian miracle," a period of double-digit economic growth and fierce repression by the country's U.S.-backed military dictatorship. The gains of this boom, Silveira recognized, were distributed unevenly: most workers had actually seen their real incomes decline, and a basic income for all Brazilians seemed to offer a means to fight increasing poverty while fueling the continued growth sought by the dictatorship and its opponents alike.

The idea was especially appealing to Workers' Party cofounder Eduardo Suplicy, who had first encountered it while completing his doctorate in economics at Michigan State University in the early 1970s. When, in 1990, Suplicy became the first PT candidate elected to the Brazilian Senate, he used his national platform to advance basic income. Months after taking office, he introduced the first version of what would ultimately become the world's first national law guaranteeing all citizens the right to a basic income, beginning with those in greatest need. Suplicy's bill entailed a radical rethinking of the Brazilian social safety net, which since the midcentury presidency of corporatist Getúlio Vargas had centered on the half of Brazilian workers employed in the formal sector. The benefits that Suplicy proposed, in contrast, would be universal, owed to all Brazilians by virtue of their citizenship or permanent residency.

Suplicy's 1991 bill never passed, but it presaged the political ferment that would characterize the Brazilian 1990s. The country had just left behind two decades of dictatorship and enacted a remarkably progressive constitution in 1988, and new social and intellectual currents were churning fast. These were the doings not only of politicians linked to the PT and other formal parties, but also to social movements pursuing diverse if often interrelated iterations of collectivism.

The effort to democratize the economy through collective forms of production was not new in the world, nor unique to Brazil. The initiatives developed by Robert Owen in the nineteenth century gave rise to cooperatives, the classical form of what has come to be called the solidarity economy. The particular forms that these collectives assumed in Brazil were heavily influenced by the ideas of Austro-Brazilian economist and PT luminary Paul Singer. The need to sustain a large body of workers excluded from the formal labor market helped economic collectives take root in Brazil and elsewhere, offering shared access to production, distribution, consumption, savings, and credit. In the 1990s and beyond, they came to include informal production groups, collective management of businesses that had failed during successive financial crises, farm unions to secure a better position in the market, community management of joint finances, and even mechanisms to include individuals with mental health challenges. What joined these initiatives were the principles of collective management, the sharing of profits, and the commitment to decent jobs for all workers.

Each of these initiatives had its origins in the self-organization of civil society, and together they reshaped the practices of social movements, unions, and neighborhood associations. At a time marked by the fall of the Berlin Wall and the collapse of Soviet socialism, the solidarity economy became the programmatic reserve of left-wing parties and movements at the margins of capitalism. Support from successive governments, from small municipalities to the 2003–10 administration of the first Workers' Party president, Luiz Inácio Lula da Silva, deepened the reach of these measures and diversified their modes of action.

Perhaps the clearest example of this phenomenon is the community bank. In the late 1990s, the residents of a poor community in the city of Fortaleza, a tropical tourist destination with underdeveloped infrastructure, formed a community association and launched a bank offering small loans to neighborhood businesses. Inspired by Singer's ideas and by liberation theology, community leaders founded a bank in the same vein as Nobel laureate Muhammad Yunus's Grameen Bank in Bangladesh. The initiative, soon named Banco Palmas, grew quickly. Through its practice of collective management, the bank created its own local currency, the palma, to ensure that shared resources remained within the community. This social currency proved an enormous success, in part because it was pegged to the real and thus offered meaningful security to local businesses.

Federal authorities moved quickly to limit the circulation of the palmas, only changing course and developing a regulatory framework for the currency after Lula's election. This was a joint effort of the Brazilian central bank and the National Secretariat of the Solidarity Economy, a new agency led by Singer himself. Singer passed away in 2018, leaving behind a richly theorized model of cooperativism that, while often overlooked in public debate, has reshaped life in countless communities. Today, Banco Palmas presides over a network of more than a hundred community banks and social currencies, the most extensive in the world.

As community banking took root in the late 1990s and early 2000s, social policy began to shift as well. In 1997 a new federal program offered to subsidize local basic income initiatives, and a growing number of state and municipal authorities, taking advantage of this, began offering cash for parents who sent their children to school. In 2001 this was further expanded with federal guarantees to support such programs completely. Sensing opportunity, Suplicy reintroduced his basic income bill that year. Three years later, Lula signed a modified version into law. The measure promised Brazilian citizens and permanent residents the right to a monthly income with no restrictions, beginning with those most in need and to be expanded within the bounds of budgetary constraints.

The day after sanctioning Suplicy's law, Lula signed into law the first step toward a guaranteed income, the now-famous Bolsa Família. Implemented on a scale unmatched by previous federal social programs, Bolsa Família has proven remarkably effective, helping to slash the share of Brazilians living below the World Bank's international poverty line from 9.7 percent to 2.7 percent in its first decade. In recent years, the program, like the country's community banking network, has survived the 2016 coup against Lula's successor, Dilma Rouseff, and the concomitant rise of Brazil's radical right, which has used Bolsa Familia as a lightning rod. There is no more striking case study than Bolsonaro, who clearly detests the program and has cut more beneficiaries than in any previous administration, yet who also added a thirteenth annual payment around the holidays, a standard formal-sector benefit. While ever more precarious, the state of Bolsa Família, like the proliferation of social currencies, shows that the terrain on which Brazilian social policy is debated has shifted meaningfully since the millennium.

AFTER AN EXPEDITION along the coast of Brazil in 1503, the navigator Amerigo Vespucci returned to Europe, noting in the account of his voyage that he had discovered a group of islands lush enough to convince him that "paradise is here." It is common in Brazil to say that this line from Vespucci about the Fernando de Noronha archipelago, now a national park, is what inspired Thomas More's description of Utopia in 1516.

While Vespucci's islands are more than 1,200 miles from Rio, Maricá still fits More's story, and not only because of its coastal mountains and many lagoons: like More's Utopia, Maricá now figures prominently in economic and philosophical debates about just societies.

The set of initiatives taken by the city, basic income among them, has given Maricá a new claim to the nickname the City of Utopias. It is undeniable that extraordinary income from offshore petroleum reserves has made a bold vision of the future possible for the city. But it is also true that other Brazilian municipalities that have seen new oil revenues, including in the state of Rio, were not able to formulate or implement a project capable of altering the typical course of predatory resource extraction and its negative externalities.

All of this is directly connected to the personal trajectory of Washington Quaquá, the first PT mayor elected to govern Maricá. A charismatic political leader with an unusual history, even by the standards of the Latin American left, Quaquá was born in Maricá's favelas. Elected in 2008 and reelected four years later, Quaquá's administration coincided with a favorable economic moment, a period often referred to as the "second Brazilian miracle." He seized the opportunity to advance a vision of political transformation grounded in a proprietary mix of collectivism, class struggle, and pragmatism. His approach was heavily informed by Singer and Suplicy, with basic income, community banking, and a dramatic infrastructural overhaul at its heart.

For Quaquá's transformative social experiment to succeed, the popular conception of Maricá as a poor, inhospitable, unattractive place in the shadow of the Marvelous City, Rio, would have to change. Few were as invested in this state of affairs as the bus monopoly responsible for shuttling residents back and forth between Maricá and Rio. Because regional cities such as Maricá have typically had little or no wealth generation, contractors in garbage collection, food distribution, and transportation have long offered local elites an opportunity to earn consistently outsize profits. Taking direct aim at this system, in 2014 Quaquá instituted a free public bus network within the city. The move brought the city national attention, enraging local elites while earning deep praise from residents, who rely on public transportation to cross a sprawling municipality of 140 square miles.

Quaquá dedicated himself to consolidating his project through the election four years later of his successor, Fabiano Horta, also from the PT. It was during Horta's term that the policies launched by Quaquá reached full scale. This was especially true of the city's basic income program, which is a global flagship. First launched in 2013, the policy initially offered payments of 85 mumbucas to households listed in the Cadastro Único, Brazil's unified register for social benefits. As the basic income program expanded, the monthly payments increased to 130 mumbucas, and additional benefits were offered to pregnant women, students, and indigenous residents. By June 2019, some 14,000 lower-income households were receiving the benefit.

That month, Horta oversaw the largest expansion of the program yet. The 130 mumbuca payment, the city announced, would now be made to individuals, not households. To qualify, individuals needed to be registered in the Cadastro Único, belong to households earning less than three times the Brazilian minimum salary, and have lived in Maricá for three years. Following a concerted registration drive in late 2019, the program's rolls swelled to more than 42,000 individuals. Each of Maricá's 42,000 basic income beneficiaries now receives a sum equivalent to R$1,560 per year, or 4.5 percent of Brazil's per capita GDP. (By point of contrast, the value of the annual dividend paid by the closest thing to a minimum income program in the United States, the Alaska Permanent Fund, ranges from 1.5 to 3 percent of Alaska's per capita GDP.) In the aggregate, the program injects R$5.5 million into the local economy each month, all of which must be spent in the city of Maricá.

Fossil fuel revenue is by nature unsustainable, fiscally and environmentally. While oil production and royalty disbursement are the domains of Petrobras and the federal government, Maricá has sought to mitigate the attendant fiscal instability by creating its own municipal sovereign wealth fund. Launched in late 2017, the fund has already achieved a total value of R$285 million ($55 million) and is projected to exceed R$1 billion in the next decade. The fund offers a platform for the city, in which a sizeable share of the population lives in poverty, to enter the financial market on favorable terms, and as it grows, the income it generates will enable the city to lower costs of capital for critical development projects while guaranteeing key social programs in perpetuity. This model has broad applicability, and not only in places experiencing commodity booms, as recent proposals for municipal "coronabonds" in the United States illustrate.

The response to the COVID-19 crisis will have a determinative impact on political processes around the world. This is doubly true in Brazil, where Maricá's anticipatory measures against the virus, announced before a single case had been recorded there, are diametrically opposed to the denialism and cruelty of Bolsonaro's federal government. Beyond downplaying the danger of COVID-19 and urging the abandonment of social distancing for the sake of the economy, the government was also timid in the face of growing demands for social protection on the part of the population, leading a national coalition of civil society organizations to successfully push Congress for a basic income in the mold of Maricá.

As the opportunities for emergency response opened by Maricá's embrace of basic income and the solidarity economy reveal, policies built in the present can open or close the space available to policymakers for decades. Our responses to the COVID-19 crisis, in Brazil as in the United States and elsewhere, will help determine the shape of the world to come. Let's be sure that the policy choices we make now drive us, not toward reinvestment in individualism and greed, but toward a deepening of cooperation and solidarity.

NO ONE IS DISPOSABLE

COVID-19 AND THE POLITICS OF DISPOSABILITY

Shaun Ossei-Owusu

IN THE FINAL CHAPTER of his 1992 book *Faces at the Bottom of the Well: The Persistence of Racism*, Derrick Bell, Harvard Law School's first tenured Black professor, describes a fictional world eerily similar to the one we know today. Local and federal governments ostensibly have no money. "Decades of conservative, laissez-faire capitalism had emptied the coffers of all but a few of the very rich," the narrator says. Because of a host of poor choices, the country "was struggling to survive like any third-world nation," and financial exigencies "curtailed all but the most necessary services." The parallels are acute: "the environment was in shambles, as reflected by the fact that the sick and elderly had to wear special masks whenever they ventured out-of-doors."

In the story, English-speaking extraterrestrial beings land on the shores of New Jersey and offer to solve everything: gold to bail out companies, chemicals to clean the environment. The country can have this deal for one sweet price: "all the African Americans who lived in the United States." This is the central, controversial claim in Bell's work of science fiction: that white people would sell Black people to aliens for the right price. The story concludes with a successful trade. Twenty million Black men, women, and children are stripped to just one undergarment, lined up, chained, and whisked away, like many of their ancestors' centuries before.

Bell's story lays bare the politics of disposability. But unlike the world of the story, the world of COVID-19 is not divided solely into Black and white. It is also white and non-white; poor and not poor; essential and nonessential; white collar and blue collar; Asian and not Asian; undocumented and citizen; able-bodied and sick; young and elderly; first-generation college students and blue bloods; free and imprisoned; celebrities with access to instant testing and plebeians; red states and blue states; and countless other binaries. From these overlapping inequities, we get a glimpse of who is disposable: the people who occupy any of the wrong categories. The scholar and cultural critic Henry Giroux analyzes this politics in his book *Against the Terror of Neoliberalism* (2008). "It is a politics in which the unproductive (the poor, weak and racially marginalized) are considered useless and therefore expendable," Giroux writes, and "in which entire populations are considered disposable, unnecessary burdens on state coffers, and consigned to fend for themselves."

Tragically, demographic data about COVID-19 deaths have borne out this vision. In April Kaiser Health News was among the first outlets to report that "A Disproportionate Number Of African-Americans Are Dying, But The U.S. Has Been Silent On Race Data." Months later, the disproportionate death toll caused by

COVID-19 is clearer. People of color, and Black people in particular, have the highest death-to-population ratio in most states around the country. Beyond the latest numbers, we have other data points: history, what is visible from news and experience, and media accounts. These are imperfect, but they supply some information, and the implications are grim.

This is certainly *not* to say that there is some sinister grand plot to harm vulnerable populations. In Bell's allegory, intent can often be a sideshow, if not an outright distraction. The truth is more banal: systemic social inequalities have made some groups more vulnerable than others, and the question of intent is therefore irrelevant. As a criminal law professor, I teach my students that intent matters—but in reality, sometimes it doesn't. In this context, malfeasance, misguided policies, and indifference suffice. Moreover, while government is the easy and most identifiable culprit, popular complicity is at play here too, which makes this version of disposability different from Bell's telling.

The people whose disposability has been most flouted are those who work in immediate-risk industries. The financially precarious service workers out with the epidemiological wolves so the rest of society can buy groceries. The health care workers plastered on the news, who labor in a profession that tasks minority and women nurses, physician assistants, and technicians with what sociologist Adia Harvey Wingfield calls "equity work": labor that makes health institutions more available to marginalized groups. The homeless population, which was already noticeable in U.S. cities, but is now more conspicuous because of their inability to shelter in place.

Then there are the undocumented agricultural workers in the West and Southwest who can't work on Zoom like their white-collar counterparts and have now become more precious in a country that has insisted on calling them illegal. There are Native Americans—some of whom have been facing a long-standing water crisis—who have uniquely high rates of diseases that make COVID-19 more lethal. There are the Asian Americans who have been subject to hate crimes since this virus surfaced in the United States. And there are the residents in poorly serviced public housing projects in places such as Chicago, Baltimore, and my native South Bronx, where in April 2,000 public housing residents woke up to no water during an epidemic that requires vigilant hand washing.

The recent history of U.S. disasters is also telling. The Chicago heatwave of 1995 killed more than 700 people, mostly poor and elderly, and necessitated refrigerated trucks for the dead, just as happened in New York this spring. A decade later, Hurricane Katrina took the lives of more than 1,800 people in Louisiana, many of whom were poor and could not leave their homes as advised. Poor people in New York City face the same today: they do not have the benefit of escaping to second homes in Long Island and New England. And then there was Hurricane Maria, which was a little more than eighteen months ago. That disaster, which killed approximately 3,000 people in Puerto Rico, elicited similar criticisms of the federal government's slow response, and accusations that the death count was severely understated. Jason Cortés has described President Donald Trump's paper-towel-throwing spectacle during his visit to Puerto Rico as "the American commander-in-chief [choosing] to toss disposable paper to disposable people."

On Palm Sunday, Surgeon General Jerome Adams gave an ominous warning. "This is going to be the hardest and the saddest week of most Americans' lives, quite frankly," he cautioned. "This is going to be our Pearl Harbor moment, our 9/11 moment. Only, it's not going to be localized, it's going to be happening all over the country. And I want America to understand that." But who exactly has been disposed of? It certainly hasn't been all of us. Collective pronouns—the "we" and "our" and "us" of public discourse—are dangerously comforting. They give the impression of equal susceptibility, while celebrities and other prominent figures gain access to testing and top-flight health care. COVID-19 is not discriminatory as a biological matter, but history and available accounts indicate that the epidemiological fallout has been and will continue to be weighty and uneven.

During the debates about the Affordable Care Act, hysteria emerged around government-run "death panels": committees of doctors who would ration care and decide who would receive treatment. This alarm ignored the long history of rationing and unequal access to health care—the subject of Beatrix Hoffman's book *Rights and Rationing in the United States Since 1930* (2012)—but it echoes legitimate dismay about bureaucrats making decisions about who lives and who dies. People with disabilities, racial minorities, undocumented immigrants, prisoners, and the poor did not figure prominently in the frenzy around death panels, but they have reason to be worried now. The uninsured, elderly, and an ever-growing portion of the middle class should be added to that list.

Social science data has already shown that African Americans are often denigrated, disregarded, and disbelieved by medical professionals when they claim they are in pain. Where will they fit in the treatment queues? Can we rest assured that American doctors will not take a cue from those in Italy, who deprioritized the lives of COVID-19 patients who were chronically ill, disabled, or elderly? What about the Latinx folk who constitute a third of uninsured people in the country? Bioethical scenarios usually reserved for grad school seminars are likely to be actualized.

This is not to say that rural whites have been exempt from the virus or its economic impact. COVID-19 has now worked its way into the rural and whiter parts of the country with suboptimal health care infrastructures. Rural residents live in areas that have been battered by closing hospitals, physician shortages, and poverty. Many of these people perceive themselves to be "strangers in their own land," as the title of sociologist Arlie Hochshild's 2018 book put it. Will they be disregarded too? If so, what are the electoral consequences of their political expendability, and if there turn out to be none, what does that say about the disposability of everyone else?

Bell's story struck a nerve because it highlighted the vulnerability of an entire class of people. The difference now is that the people being sacrificed extends beyond African Americans, and responsibility can be tethered not only to government but to the private sector, the media, and parts of the general public. The outcome of this story is uncertain. But when the dust settles, there will be a tale to tell of who mattered and who was sacrificed.

COVID-19 AND THE COLOR LINE

Colin Gordon, Walter Johnson,
Jason Q. Purnell, & Jamala Rogers

AS THE COVID-19 CRISIS unfolds, its toll on African Americans is coming into sharper focus. In almost every setting, African Americans are contracting the virus—and dying from it—at startlingly disproportionate rates. In Alabama, African Americans account for 27 percent of the population, 44 percent of COVID-19 cases, and 45 percent of COVID-19 deaths. In Illinois, African Americans account for 14 percent of the population, 22 percent of COVID-19 cases, and 28 percent of COVID-19 deaths. In Wisconsin, African Americans account for just 6 percent of the population but nearly a quarter of COVID-19 deaths. Starkest of all, in the city of St. Louis, African Americans account for 47 percent of the population, almost 60 percent of COVID-19 cases, and over two thirds of those who have died.

How do we account for this damage, for what *New York Times* columnist Charles Blow aptly dubbed the racial time bomb at the heart of the COVID-19 crisis? The answer to that question has deep and tangled historical roots. It is a story not just of discrimination, but of systematic exploitation, exclusion, subordination, and predation. The ability to live a long and healthy life is predicated on access to a range of social and economic resources systematically denied African American families and communities. In St. Louis, as elsewhere, African American workers are overrepresented among frontline service workers, among whom low wages are the rule and the luxury of social distancing is not. In order to get to work, or even to shop at a grocery store, many must spend hours on public transportation. Because health care in our society is generally allocated according to employment, it is least accessible to those who need it the most. In St. Louis, African Americans are more than twice as likely as whites to be uninsured. Without economic security or options, and without adequate protection on the job, these workers and their communities have been delivered to disease by their history—by U.S. history.

The slow violence that we see unfolding in St. Louis has been structured into the fabric of the city, built brick-by-brick by those who have sought profit in segregation and comfort in social distance. Its racialized patterns of disadvantage are the result of decades of conscious choices by actors at every level of government, aided and abetted by private industries such as banking, insurance, and real estate, to name but a few. St. Louis's history of imposed Black deprivation is both unique to it and reflective of the broader patterns that have made COVID-19 a charnel house for Black Americans nationwide.

WHITE ST. LOUIS has been in a sort of self-imposed social distancing for most of the century. In 1916 it passed a racial zoning law by popular referendum. After the Supreme Court struck down racial zoning on equal protection grounds the next year (in *Buchanan v. Warley*), St. Louis realtors, developers, and homeowners turned to the use of racial restrictions written into property deeds—"covenants" that bound neighborhoods and new subdivisions to whiteness. The "uniform restriction agreement" in wide use in St. Louis by the early 1930s sought to "preserve the character of said neighborhood as a desirable place of residence for persons of the Caucasian Race," holding that homeowners could not "erect, maintain, operate, or permit to be erected, maintained or operated any slaughterhouse, junk shop or rag-picking establishment" or "sell, convey, lease, or rent to a negro or negroes." These restrictions, written into the deed as a condition of sale, still turn up in property transactions all over the city today.

By the end of the 1940s, such agreements prohibited the "nuisance" of Black occupancy in nearly a third of the city's housing stock. For realtors and landlords, these covenants were money in the bank. On the white side of the lines, they could extract a premium price by promising that the new resident or renter would never need to worry about having a Black neighbor. On the Black side of the line, they could extract ever-higher rents from a population that was growing through the years of the Great Migration (the massive movement of African Americans from the South in the first half of the twentieth century), but legally confined to a few areas of the city. It was in Black St. Louis that the real money was to be made: slicing up buildings into ever-smaller kitchenette apartments while skimping on upkeep and improvement. At the time of World War II, indoor plumbing was still rare in many of the Black neighborhoods in St. Louis.

In 1948 the Supreme Court, in a case originating in St. Louis (*Shelley v. Kraemer*), declared that restrictive covenants were legally unenforceable. (Only six of the nine justices voted—the other three recused themselves because they, too, lived in covenanted racial enclaves.) Segregation, however, remained. Increasingly, it took the form of federal, state, and local subsidies that were in reality available almost exclusively to whites—for example, G.I. Bill housing benefits available only to white veterans and Federal Housing Association loan guarantees distributed according to racist protocols in a pattern that has come to be known as "redlining." This meant that loan guarantees were hived off from neighborhoods where Blacks lived, while white St. Louis expanded into the emerging suburban frontier in St. Louis County. Whites moved west along an unfolding network of interstate highways, which were themselves an economic subsidy to whiteness—built by white construction workers through Black neighborhoods for the purpose of making it easier for white suburbanites to get to work downtown.

As well as by police harassment and vigilante violence, Black mobility into the suburbs was limited by the seemingly mundane tools of municipal incorporation and land-use zoning. "White flight" suburbs popped up like mushrooms west of the city (there are almost ninety municipalities in St. Louis County today). Many of these brand-new cities had zoning codes which excluded multifamily dwellings and stipulated large minimum sizes for home lots, thus ensuring that only the right sort of people (read: comparatively wealthy and almost entirely white) could move in. To this day, many of the municipalities in the broad westward corridor out of the city are 95 percent (or more) white. While similar patterns of white flight and urban decline unfolded elsewhere—indeed, this is the enduring pattern of U.S. life—St. Louis was its apotheosis. "St. Louis is not a typical city," as one reporter noted in the late 1970s, "but, like a Eugene O'Neill play, it shows a general condition in stark and dramatic form."

The mutually exacerbating patterns of federal preference and municipal connivance were reinforced by the state government of Missouri—a Confederate-claimed and Jim Crow state in which social, economic, and tax policy have been shaped by a long history of systematic racism. Like all slaveholding states, Missouri was reluctant to tax property. This left many of its cities and towns without the capacity to sustain decent public goods and services—a constraint exaggerated by the 1980 Hancock Amendment, which put a hard cap on property tax increases. And, like most southern states, Missouri underdeveloped its social safety net, underfunding education, paring eligibility and benefits in federal–state unemployment and cash assistance programs, and recently declining to expand Medicaid coverage under the Affordable Care Act.

Over the second half of the twentieth century, St. Louis became—and now remains—one of the most segregated cities in the country. The so-called "Delmar Divide" splits St. Louis into two worlds: north of that line (over 97 percent African American by 1970), the housing stock has crumbled, economic opportunities have vanished, and public goods—especially schools—are scarce and deteriorating. Today, you can map virtually any index of social well-being—rates of childhood asthma, access to broadband, level of education upon leaving school, life expectancy—and a stark disparity will be evident along the east–west path of Delmar Boulevard.

Many in Black St. Louis point to the early 1970s as the beginning of the end for North City. In response to a 1973 RAND Corporation report, future U.S. congressman and Democratic presidential candidate Richard Gephardt introduced to the Board of Aldermen a motion declaring North St. Louis "an insignificant residential area not worthy of special maintenance effort." Gephardt's brazen indifference was developed by the urban planning firm Team 4 into a comprehensive plan for the city that recommended a strategy of "triage": continuing investment in thriving areas of the city, targeted investment in "marginal areas," and abandonment of the North Side. The report provoked widespread outrage and was officially disavowed by the city—but it is, in effect, exactly what happened. In 1979, in the face of widespread public outcry and sustained street-level resistance, the city closed Homer G. Phillips Hospital, which had served the North Side since the 1930s, and had gained a national reputation for Black medical excellence. It was, one of the white city leaders explained in justifying the closing, too hard to get all way up there from city hall.

As the city rapidly deteriorated, those African Americans who could afford to do so tried to migrate to the inner-ring suburbs of central and north St. Louis County. They were met with overt hostility and sustained resistance. The city of Ferguson, to give only a single example, considered building a ten-foot wall along the entirety of its border with the majority-Black city of Kinloch—*in 1976*. Gradually, these suburbs were integrated, and thus began a second wave of federally subsidized white flight along widened interstates pushing farther and farther west away from the city.

IT IS THIS HISTORY—of white cupidity supported at every level of government and woven into the fabric of daily life—that has rendered up African Americans in St. Louis and St. Louis County to the virus. "The resources that are necessary to live a long and productive life are not equally distributed throughout the St. Louis region," as a comprehensive report on *Segregation in St. Louis* concluded in 2018. "They are not randomly distributed either. This unequal distribution of opportunity is the result of decades of policy at the local, state, and federal levels of government, and it is reinforced by systems, institutions, and industries . . . that reproduce unequal outcomes."

As investment, economic development, and employment followed the highways west, the combination of sustained segregation and dramatic deindustrialization in Greater St. Louis ensured that while capital could move, the African American working class could not. The scattering of jobs that remained offered lower wages, fewer benefits, or long and expensive commutes. The median income of African Americans in Greater St. Louis is half that of white median income, while the rates of poverty and unemployment are three times as great. Since 1980, by one estimate, the incomes of young Black men in the city of St. Louis have fallen from $29,443 to just over $11,000.

All this comes with physical risks because health is the result of more than the availability of health care. Health—like economic mobility—is deeply influenced by place, causing public health experts to note that zip code is more determinative of health outcomes than genetic code. African Americans in St. Louis are *twelve times* more likely than white residents to live in neighborhoods of concentrated poverty, which often contain environmental risks, including poor air or water quality, industrial toxins, and the failure of sanitary infrastructure. These are the sources of heightened rates of respiratory and other illnesses among African Americans. And these are the reasons that the life expectancy of residents of North St. Louis is eighteen years shorter than it is for residents of suburban Clayton, less than ten miles away. Such conditions compound other political, social, and economic disadvantages, which undermine access not just to economic opportunity, but to adequate social services, decent schools, and nutritious food.

One of the starkest tragedies of these neighborhoods is that they crush social mobility; their residents are "stuck in place." According to research by Raj Chetty and colleagues, growing up poor in St. Louis correlates with an annual loss of nearly $4,000 in adult incomes and a razor-thin chance of moving up in the income distribution (a metric on which St. Louis ranks 2,419 out of 2,478 counties in the United States). Most children born into a North St. Louis zip code will die in that same place. These are tragedies, but they are not accidents. They are the wrongs of the past, ramifying generation after generation, the fruit of two and a half centuries of policy and practice.

The moral condition of a society, it is often said, is clearest in the condition of its prisons, and it is in St. Louis's criminal justice system that the long fetch of history is most brutally evident. The

Department of Justice's 2015 investigation of the Ferguson Police Department painstakingly documents the climate of abuse and police impunity that places African Americans—especially young Black men—in mortal danger. In the determination of police and courts—especially in the county's struggling suburbs—to use fines and forfeitures to keep the lights on at city hall, we see the region's history of segregation and state subsidy of whiteness converted into an occasion to extract *even more wealth* from poor Blacks.

The result of this final round of extraction is an obscene racial disparity in incarceration rates: in the city, African Americans are locked up at eight times the rate of whites (in the county, the disparity is about five to one). A staggering number of those behind bars in the city's notorious "workhouse" (as well as in a host of other lockups throughout the county) have been charged with nonviolent misdemeanors and are still awaiting a court date. They are presumed innocent, but are too poor to pay the fines levied against them for petty municipal offenses or code violations.

IN ST. LOUIS, as in the country at large, the deadly disparities of the pandemic are as unsurprising as they are unsettling. It is not simply that African Americans in St. Louis, as in the rest of the United States, have been left behind, and thus set in the way of the virus. They have been *offered up* by a history of racist privilege and profiteering—from prisons to poor neighborhoods, from persistent segregation to willful policy failure.

In 1857 Supreme Court chief justice Roger B. Taney infamously denied standing to Dred Scott, a free Black man who had returned to Missouri and sued to retain his freedom. Taney ruled that Black Americans "are not included, and were not intended to be included, under the word 'citizens' in the Constitution, and can therefore claim none of the rights and privileges which that instrument provides for and secures." One can only view the subsequent history of St. Louis (and of Missouri, and of the United States), and its consequences in our current moment, and wonder at how little has changed.

WHY HAS COVID-19 NOT LED TO MORE HUMANITARIAN RELEASES?

Dan Berger

IN 1971, two weeks shy of his twentieth birthday, Anthony Bottom, a young Black Panther, along with another Panther, Albert Nuh Washington, were arrested following a shootout with San Francisco police. The pair would be tried along with a third man, Herman Bell, for a separate attack: the May killing of two New York City police officers. They were convicted and sentenced to twenty-five years to life, the maximum penalty in New York at the time. The judge said the sentence was befitting a society at war.

Bottom had first joined the Panthers in the weeks immediately following the assassination of Martin Luther King, Jr. In prison, Bottom converted to Islam and adopted a new name, Jalil Muntaqim. After almost five decades of incarceration, Muntaqim has racked up a laudatory file of accomplishments. He earned two bachelor's degrees before Bill Clinton ended Pell eligibility for incarcerated people. He cofounded an organization, the Jericho Movement, dedicated to the release of U.S. political prisoners. He has received numerous accolades from human rights organizations for his dedication to social justice. He has taught poetry, history, and alternatives to violence classes for other incarcerated people. When I first began corresponding with him nearly two decades ago, he was organizing a fundraiser for AIDS orphans in Africa.

In 2002 Muntaqim became eligible for parole. Yet the Patrolmen's Benevolence Association—the revanchist police fraternity that has shielded abusive cops and pursued aggressive forms of social control—lobbied heavily against it, as it has every time he has come up for parole. The PBA even set up a website to monitor the schedule of parole hearings for anyone convicted of killing a police officer, allowing visitors to send an automatically generated letter to the parole board opposing consideration of release.

For decades the PBA effectively controlled the parole board, and such pressure ensured Muntaqim would be denied parole every two years. Each time he has been denied parole, the board has stated that its decision is based not on his deeds in prison or his readiness for release, but on the nature of his crime. Since that can never change, PBA pressure renders the parole board irrelevant. Every prison sentence becomes a de facto death penalty—as became evident when one of Muntaqim's codefendants, Albert Nuh Washington, was denied compassionate release for stage IV liver cancer. He died in a prison hospital in April 2000.

When COVID-19 struck, Muntaqim's advocates argued before the state that his life was in grave peril. Fourteen of the top twenty pandemic outbreak clusters have been in prisons and jails, and incarceration creates and exacerbates a number of health problems.

At sixty-eight years old, having lived for fifty years in prison—and having survived a stroke, hypertension, and heart disease—Muntaqim is at extreme risk of dying from COVID-19. He is one of more than 9,000 people over the age of 55 who is incarcerated in New York. An estimated 10 percent of the nation's prison population is in this high-risk age group. Yet governors have thus far refused to act on clemency for elderly people.

Recognizing the precarious situation, the New York State Supreme Court ordered Muntaqim's temporary release at the end of April. In granting it, Judge Stephan Schick said, "Mr. Muntaqim may have gotten a 25-to-life sentence, but it was not a death sentence." The state Black, Puerto Rican, Hispanic, and Asian Legislative Caucus agreed, offering a letter of support for his release. Yet the state—led by Attorney General Letitia James, the first Black woman to occupy that role—appealed Sullivan's ruling. As the appeal wound its way through the courts, Muntaqim sickened. On May 25 he was transferred to the Albany Medical Hospital with COVID-19. Ten days later, with damage to one of his lungs, his kidneys, and liver, Muntaqim had recovered enough to be transferred back to the prison infirmary. That same day, June 4, the Appellate Division reversed Judge Schick's ruling. Muntaqim, the court said, must remain in prison.

New York's intransigence fits with a national pattern that the pandemic has revealed. For while a number of municipalities shrank their jail admissions in the early months of the pandemic, no state has meaningfully reduced its prison population. Jails generally house people who are awaiting trial but who are too poor to make bail or who are serving short sentences, whereas prisons house people who have been found guilty and sentenced to a year or more. In the restrictive purview of elite empathy, then, jails have been an easier sell for massive reduction. According to an analysis by the Prison Policy Initiative, local municipalities have reduced their jail populations by an average of 31 percent. State governments and the federal Bureau of Prisons, meanwhile, have reduced their incarcerated population by an average of just 5 percent. Typically this has meant a release of a few hundred people—some of whom have not been released but merely transferred to home confinement.

A number of states have created an almost nonexistent category of those warranting release: people over fifty-five who are serving time for nonviolent drug offenses and who are within three months of release. Yet few of the many septuagenarians in our nation's prisons meet this restrictive categorization. As the group Release Aging People in Prison (RAPP) noted in its evaluation when New York governor Andrew Cuomo created this impossible category, 98 percent of the people over 55 incarcerated in New York are excluded from consideration for release under Cuomo's plan.

Meanwhile New York prisons remain the epicenter of the outbreak in the state. As of July 9, the state Department of Corrections and Community Supervision reports 1,300 prison staff and 545 incarcerated people have tested positive for the disease. (The actual numbers are likely higher.) Yet due to low levels of testing, the comorbidities of incarceration, and the generally abysmal levels of health care inside, four times as many incarcerated people as staff die from the pandemic. And the vast majority of those who have died have been Black or Latinx—higher even than the already disparate rates at which New Yorkers of color outside of prison have succumbed to the pandemic. RAPP calculates that 81 percent of the deaths in prison since the pandemic began, both related to COVID-19 and not, have been people of color. Black people account for 14 percent of New York state, 50 percent of the state's prison population, but 60 percent of the deaths since the pandemic began.

And it is not just New York. Washington governor Jay Inslee has been widely praised for his commitment to science-based responses to climate change and the pandemic. Yet even in a proclamation declaring that elderly people are at particular risk of contracting the pandemic and that prisons are too crowded for people to practice effective social distancing, Inslee only committed to releasing a few hundred people from a state prison system that confines 19,000. Inslee's order pertained only to those who fall into the elusive category that political scientist Marie Gottschalk has called the "non-non-nons": nonviolent, non-serious, non-sexual offenses. Inslee added a further narrowing claim that required people to be within three months of their release. In Pennsylvania, advocates grew so weary of Governor Tom Wolf's refusal to engage in widespread releases that they launched a hunger strike on June 1.

Governors nationwide have pursued similarly limited initiatives. This is the reform conjured by focus groups and vetted by police unions, not the one backed by data. Five decades of mass incarceration has so thoroughly limited the imagination of political elites that even a pandemic cannot dislodge their belief in the necessity of mass incarceration. Their refusal of a broad humanitarian release of incarcerated senior citizens serving lengthy sentences—really the lowest of bars—reveals, in its absurd perverseness, a deeper truth: even the most liberal of U.S. governors would rather risk their prisons turning into mass graves than offer the faintest of admissions that mass incarceration is a colossal failure and unnecessary for public safety.

If liberal politicians struggle to admit this fact, conservative politicians continue to run in the opposite direction, insisting that the carceral state alone stands between civilization and chaos, despite all evidence to the contrary. In a speech that branded Antifa—an umbrella term for antifascism activists—domestic terrorism, Attorney General William Barr menaced would-be demonstrators by saying, "It is a federal crime to cross state lines or to use interstate facilities to incite or participate in violent rioting." He promised to "enforce these laws." The law in question is part of the 1968 repressive Anti-Riot Act that was appended to the otherwise laudatory Fair Housing Act. Legislators rushed to pass this bill after King's assassination and the tinderbox it lit nationwide; they colloquially referred to their repressive cri de coeur as the H. Rap Brown bill, after the charismatic leader of SNCC.

The carceral state is anticipatory violence masquerading as responsive force, and Barr has been preparing for this moment for a long time. Last August, Barr praised police as "fighting an unrelenting, never-ending" war and deserving of "ticker-tape parades." Barr has actually made it harder for incarcerated people to get out of federal prison during the pandemic and then placed the whole federal prison system in lockdown. Yet he was quick to criminalize the nationwide protests against police violence. He promised to utilize the Joint

Terrorism Task Force (JTTF), a collaboration between federal and local police that began in 1980 to stop a rash of bank robberies (including those allegedly committed by the Black Liberation Army). This amounts to a federal redefinition of any protest against police as terrorism. The nation's jails and prisons stand ready to detain the latest targets of America's long war.

Police departments heard the message clearly, as they have targeted largely nonviolent demonstrations with a seemingly endless amount of tear gas, flash grenades, clubs, tanks, pepper spray, and mace. What we have witnessed is a national police riot, complete with numerous actions that would qualify as war crimes. New York police clubbed peaceful demonstrators, then charged at them with SUVs (this has been reported in Boston as well). In Philadelphia police cordoned demonstrators onto the highway and then gassed them all with no place to escape. Later, other officers posed for photographs with armed white vigilantes. Washington, D.C., police shot tear gas inside a private residence after the homeowner sheltered fleeing demonstrators. Louisville police had no body cameras on when they shot and killed a Black restauranteur who frequently served police. Around the country, police have obscured their badge numbers before engaging in unceasing violence. All this in stark contrast to the muted response police gave armed white reactionaries at state houses just weeks before. The police, writes critic Alex Parene, have taken the side of white vigilantes.

Meanwhile Muntaqim and hundreds of thousands of other incarcerated people have been abandoned to the courts and COVID-19. In the face of federal threats to break the backs of protestors, though, the actions against state violence continue. By returning daily to the streets, violating curfews, seizing hotels shuttered by COVID-19, caring for each other amidst a pandemic and a rampaging police state, and pulling down racist statutes, thousands of Americans display heroic courage. They are willing to give their lives to the work of remaking the country by ending policing and incarceration as we know them. Spontaneous uprisings are by nature unpredictable, yet a cogent demand is emerging from coast to coast: "Defund the police." Every day in the streets of U.S. cities and towns, these rebellions seek to overturn the police state that consolidated in opposition to Muntaqim and other Black radicals of the 1960s. For in moving to defund police, we must also act to dismantle the prison system where many victims of police violence reside.

MOTHERING IN A PANDEMIC

Anne L. Alstott

AS THE CRISIS IN THE BUSINESS SECTOR occupies Congress, the quieter crisis in many U.S. homes goes largely unnoticed. In theory, all parents of young children must now navigate a world without schools and daycare. But, in practice, the heaviest burden falls on mothers, especially single ones, who face a near-impossible choice between caring for their children and staying afloat financially.

Despite some progress toward gender equality, mothers in different-sex couples still do the lion's share of childcare. Most mothers, even those with babies and toddlers, now hold paid jobs, but even so, mothers bear the heaviest burden. They not only do the greater share of hands-on care, but they also tend to take on what we might call child management: the work of arranging for childcare and filling in when those arrangements fall through. When the babysitter is sick, the daycare is closed, or school vacation rolls around, it is primarily mothers who must scramble for alternatives—or sacrifice their own work to stay at home. These dynamics persist even when both mothers and fathers work full time. Women also take on the greatest load of caring for elderly family members and for people who are sick—including COVID-19 victims.

We can hope that the pandemic will actually help equalize parenting roles, at least in two-parent families. With both mom and dad on site 24/7, perhaps they will hash out a more egalitarian division of labor. But that rosy scenario must be balanced against the reality that married mothers in different-sex couples tend to have lower-paid and lower-status jobs. Even with the best of intentions, couples may find that the economic threat of the pandemic intensifies the personal, professional, and social dynamics that lead couples to give priority to the father's job and working time over the mother's.

In a personal essay on Slate, Emily Gould captures why these decisions feel rational, even necessary in a time of crisis. "Our long-term stability as a family hinges on whether my husband can do the work he needs to do this year in order to keep his salaried job," she writes. "If there is only enough time for one of us to work, it doesn't make sense for that person to be me."

The gendered impact of the pandemic falls hardest on the 8 million mothers who are raising children alone. Single mothers tend to earn low wages, to work in service occupations, and to have limited access to benefits such as health insurance and pensions. At the same time, they have principal, and often sole, responsibility for the care of their children. Many have little or no financial support from the nonresident parent.

Single mothers now face a personal—and nonetheless tragic—choice. With schools closed and daycare shuttered, children need a parent at home. But a single mother who stays home can risk eviction and starvation: without a paycheck, the rent goes unpaid, and groceries are unaffordable. These risks are most pressing for the lowest-paid workers. But as the lockdown continues, more and more white-collar mothers, too, will find themselves without a paycheck if they cannot work. Going to work—if childcare can somehow be found—now poses a literal physical danger not only to the woman but to her children as well.

Although the tradeoff between personal safety and a paycheck now confronts many workers, single mothers face an especially high-stakes choice because of their children. Child trauma experts point out that the pandemic has imposed great stress on children. Quarantine has disrupted children's routines. In some places children cannot even play outside. At the same time, shelter-in-place protocols have cut off children from their friends, their teachers, and their extended family. In some cases of shared custody, the pandemic has cut off children from their nonresident parent.

From an adult's perspective, these schedule disruptions may seem small and temporary. Surely kids will enjoy a break from school and a few extra hours of screen time. And, after all, it's we adults who have to worry about the big stuff, like jobs and putting food on the table. But from a child's perspective, the disruptions caused by quarantine are not minor matters. Younger children's developing bodies and brains need predictability and routine as well as productive stimulation. And older children may worry intensely about the danger of COVID-19 to themselves and their families.

Nor is the COVID-19 experience just a short-term blip of stress that will necessarily fade when the pandemic threat wanes in a year or eighteen months. Some children will bounce back with no ill effects, but the science of trauma suggests that some children may experience biological changes that pose long-term risks for their physical and mental health. Harvard's Center for the Developing Child explains:

> Toxic stress response can occur when a child experiences strong, frequent, and/or prolonged adversity—such as physical or emotional abuse, chronic neglect, caregiver substance abuse or mental illness, exposure to violence, and/or the accumulated burdens of family economic hardship—without adequate adult support. This kind of prolonged activation of the stress response systems can disrupt the development of brain architecture and other organ systems, and increase the risk for stress-related disease and cognitive impairment, well into the adult years.

The best preventative factor and remedy for children facing stress is close, reliable, and loving care by parents. We sometimes think that resilience is inborn, a character trait that people simply have or don't have. But studies show that resilience in children is strongly linked to parental care:

> The single most common factor for children who develop resilience is at least one stable and committed relationship with a supportive parent, caregiver, or other adult. These relationships provide the personalized responsiveness, scaffolding, and protection that buffer children from developmental disruption. They also build key capacities—such as the ability to plan, monitor, and regulate behavior—that enable children to respond adaptively to adversity and thrive.

While parental care can be supplemented by care from teachers and childcare workers, substitute care too should be warm, personalized, predictable, and supportive of each child's needs. But this kind of ideal childcare is hard to find (and to afford) even in the best of times. Cobbled-together care in a pandemic may fall woefully short.

And so the pandemic's dilemmas are especially dark for single mothers and their children. Staying at home may not be a feasible economic option, but leaving home to work may not be possible without schools and childcare. Shelter-in-place orders can also make it difficult or impossible to rely on childcare assistance from friends and relatives.

Some states and cities have begun to provide emergency childcare assistance to essential workers. But these efforts will likely be taxed by the demand. Counting only frontline health care workers, there are a stunning 4 million parents with children under the age of 14. Emergency measures of limited scope cannot feasibly replace the roles of schools, day care, and summer activities for the number of children whose parents will need to return to work to make ends meet.

The point is not just that the pandemic imposes hardship on families. That is true, but there is a deeper problem of social fairness at stake. Society relies on the unpaid, invisible work of parents—mostly mothers—to care for children and to buffer kids from trauma and stress. Today, with schools closed, mothers must step into the teachers' role as well. And the vast majority of mothers will step up, putting their children's well-being first and making whatever financial and career sacrifices they need to make. We know that's what mothers do.

But a fair society should reward rather than punish people who sacrifice their own interests for the good of society. We all share a stake in the development of the next generation. The trauma of the pandemic is very real for children, and so is the buffering effect of parental care. When mothers make sacrifices for their kids, they are performing a critical social role that allows the rest of us, quite literally, to go about our business, unencumbered by the care of the young and the vulnerable.

A fair policy response would recognize that the burden of family care will fall hardest on the parents of young children and, particularly, on mothers. But, so far, Congress has instead chosen to focus, as it did during the 2008 Great Recession, on business. Industries, from airlines to restaurants, have lined up to ask for bailouts, while benefits for families have been small, partial, and temporary.

To be sure, some business-focused policies will help mothers, but only unevenly and indirectly. The Paycheck Protection Program is far from a universal jobs guarantee, and unemployment insurance assists some but not all laid-off working parents. (Many workers are not covered because they have not worked long enough at the same job or because they work part-time.) The one-time stimulus payments of $1,200 per adult (plus $500 per child) provided welcome but short-term relief for families. Even family leave programs expanded during the pandemic provide uneven assistance: the new rules provide a mix of paid and unpaid leave for up to twelve weeks to parents who cannot work because of childcare responsibilities, but many parents will not qualify because their firms are not required to provide the leave.

A better approach would send financial relief directly to families rather than indirectly via the business sector. A universal basic income (UBI), paid for the duration of the pandemic, would provide economic security and would be simple to administer and distribute. To address the burden on families with young children, the UBI could include a supplemental payment for families with children (and other dependents who need daily care).

The UBI has most recently been championed by presidential candidate Andrew Yang as a response to technology-driven unemployment, but it is a program with a long and distinguished history—and one that could be especially valuable to mothers. The two key features of UBI are that it is universal and that it pays cash. Universality means that all families receive the money, in sharp contrast to the Paycheck Protection Program and unemployment benefits, which provide spotty coverage. With a UBI, if you are a human being, you get cash; and if you have children (or other dependents who need daily care), you get more cash.

The cash payout provided by a UBI is also especially valuable to families, because it permits parents to make choices keyed to their own, individual circumstances. Some parents would use the cash to help pay for reliable childcare and go back to work. Others would use the cash to cushion a period of staying at home with the kids. The right choice is highly individual, depending on the nature of a parent's job, the needs and ages of children, and the kind of substitute care available. These are precisely the choices that society relies on parents—especially mothers—to make, because they will, by and large, make choices that put their children first.

Although the level of UBI assistance—on the order of, say, $1,000 per month—might seem small to some, it would provide a critical baseline of economic security for single parents and for lower-earning married couples. Children benefit enormously from family stability, and a UBI could contribute directly by creating a predictable income guarantee that could lower parental stress and permit parents to make stable plans.

To be sure, a program of this size and scale would be expensive in budgetary terms. With 25 million families with children under the age of 12, a universal benefit of even $1,000 per month, paid per-family to married couples and to single parents alike, would cost $300 billion annually. Income-testing the benefits would lower the outlays needed (although at the price of introducing extra complexity into the program). Still, even though numbers like these are staggering, they are in line with the scale of relief efforts already underway. Congress's first COVID-19 relief legislation cost $2 trillion, and negotiations for more are in progress.

As small (and large) businesses line up for relief, Congress should take notice of the parents, mostly mothers, who are doing some of society's most important work by taking responsibility for children.

THE END OF FAMILY VALUES

Julie Kohler

THE COVID-19 CRISIS has been a tipping point for U.S. families. Parents are still scrambling to do their jobs under rapidly changing or even dangerous conditions while caring for children and other vulnerable loved ones. Tens of millions remain out of work with little sense of what jobs will return. The pandemic has magnified inequality and white supremacy in ways that make family life even harder. Black and Latinx Americans are contracting and dying from COVID-19 at far higher rates than white Americans. Low-wage workers and workers of color comprise the largest share of the 40 million newly unemployed. Not surprisingly, women are disproportionately shouldering increased loads of unpaid caregiving, homeschooling, and household work resulting from school closures and stay-at-home orders.

But the conditions for the squeeze that families are experiencing were set long before the pandemic hit U.S. shores. The seeming impossibility of the current situation for U.S. families is not an unfortunate byproduct of an unforeseen global health crisis. It is the inevitable result of an economic worldview that has methodically shifted more and more costs onto families' shoulders under a façade of "family values."

In recent years, critics have placed the blame for our current economic arrangement on four decades of privatization, deregulation, and tax cuts. What has received less attention are the accompanying cultural norms for families: the heightened expectations that families will provide for their own with little public support, and the assumption, sometimes implicit, that the two-parent nuclear family is the optimal family structure to do so. The two sets of norms—one economic, one cultural—are superficially distinct but deeply intertwined. In order to emerge from this crisis stronger, we must dismantle the family norms that lie at the heart of our current failed economic approach. Only then will we see the political will to invest in the kinds of public goods—from childcare to affordable higher education—that today's families need to survive and thrive.

It remains a daunting challenge. Neoliberalism's resilience does not rest on its empirical accomplishments; the United States has experienced less growth and economic security since 1980 than in the forty years prior. It endures, instead, because of its political success in advancing a vastly expanded notion of what constitutes private family responsibility and enshrining it as a "reasonable" bipartisan consensus. Moreover, one of the reasons that neoliberalism has endured politically is that it has convinced many Americans that the failure to prosper in a free and unfettered market is a personal failing—a lack of virtue stemming from poor family decision-making.

This could be the moment in which such a consensus unravels, when families' economic and time struggles become so acute and widespread that they can no longer be chalked up to poor individual choices. It is conceivable that the crisis will enable us to imagine an alternative economic future, one grounded in the recognition that families of all forms have dignity and value. Such outcomes are far from certain, but for the first time in the better part of the last half century, they are possible. The crisis is prompting a reexamination of economic tenets that have held sway for decades. Now we must do the same for the family assumptions that played an equally powerful role in neoliberalism's rise and resilience. And we must build the political institutions and power needed to make such a future a reality.

NEOLIBERALISM OWES ITS POLITICAL DOMINANCE to the common bonds forged between intellectuals, political institutions, and movement leaders. Much of the political power driving neoliberalism's rise emerged with social conservatives: the white evangelical Christian churches that, beginning in the 1970s, became increasingly politicized as a right-wing force. Neoliberal economists and social conservatives did not necessarily share a uniform view of families; as political scientist Melinda Cooper documented in *Family Values: Between Neoliberalism and the New Social Conservatism* (2017), the value of the family for economists was less about its innate moral virtue than its privatizing function. But Cooper's analysis reveals how symbiotic the two camps were. Social conservatives' reverence for the traditional nuclear family provided a values-based language to justify neoliberal efforts to dramatically erode the welfare state. And neoliberals elevated the married, two-parent family as a normative family ideal by establishing it as the basic economic unit of society—the container, so to speak, for individual economic success—and, by extension, personal virtue.

Social conservatives have not won the war of ideas when it comes to family structure; Americans today are more accepting of a wide range of family forms than at any point in history. But at the same time, the traditional family structure retains much of its cultural power due to the precarity of contemporary economic life. Thanks to a system with very little social insurance, almost no public investment in services for children outside of K-12 education, and jobs that do not pay enough to live on, individuals are in fact more tethered to families—through wealth and debt—than they were a generation ago. Families now bear near exclusive responsibility for helping provide a middle-class life for their children, through private financing of child care, an assortment of de rigueur private enrichment activities, higher education, and even eventual home ownership. As various forms of public economic support for families have been systematically eroded (e.g., cuts to public higher education, the scaling back of Pell grants) and replaced by private financing mechanisms (e.g., the expansion of private student loans), family economic ties through marriage and parenthood have been strengthened.

The net result is that family structure has become, along with race and gender, one of the prime sources of inequality in the United States. But just as a central tenet of neoliberalism is that individuals deserve the rewards and punishments they incur from largely unregulated markets, family security is framed as the result of individual choices pertaining to marriage and childbearing.

In reality, market capitalism has been advanced through a form of family capitalism that affixes different rewards and penalties to various family structures and uses the resulting discrepancies to define and reinforce the parameters of what's "normal." Married couples in the United States benefit from more than a thousand rights, benefits, and privileges they receive under federal law, whereas the United States attaches a particularly high penalty to single motherhood. Indeed, single mothers are more likely to be poor in the United States than they are in twenty-six of twenty-nine comparably rich democracies. This is not because of individual "poor lifestyle choices." Rather, it is the result of a set of policy choices, cloaked in the language of family morality, that leave single mothers more economically vulnerable in the United States than in much of the rest of the world.

Such choices do more than solidify family economic inequality; they are a tool in the maintenance of white supremacy. The policing of family structure has always been most formal and punitive for low-income families of color. Welfare reform of the 1990s, for example, was the culmination of more than thirty years of moralizing about "family breakdown" in Black communities and the stigmatizing of Black single mothers, all while simultaneously decimating families of color through mass incarceration and other forms of structural racism. Neoliberals—who included not just political conservatives such as Ronald Reagan but also "New Democrats" such as Bill Clinton—spent the better part of thirty years enacting a series of reforms designed to enforce a particular view of family morality by establishing a state interest in paternity establishment, policing child support obligations, and, in the early 2000s, promoting marriage as a solution for poverty reduction. The net effect was to transform the public interest in supporting vulnerable families into a public interest in enforcing family responsibility among low-income, disproportionately Black women.

For middle- and upper-middle-class families, the maintenance of an illusory family ideal has been more subtle and insidious. The white, married, two-parent breadwinner/homemaker family was a postwar social construction, enforced through rigid race and gender hierarchies and enabled by the family wage once paid, and the generous public housing and higher education benefits once provided, to white, largely unionized men. Over the past half century, much about families has changed. Today, 26 percent of children live with a single parent, and 61 percent of married parents with children under the age of 18 both work outside the home. Yet there has been no commensurate reduction in caregiving and household labor and few new public supports to help families manage the responsibilities that were once relegated to full-time homemakers. Nor is there any formal support—in the form of tax, monetary, housing, or other policy—for the kinds of family structures that would be better equipped to manage the responsibilities of a neoliberal economy, such as extended family or fictive kin networks.

"We're living with the household requirements of the 1960s but the work and parenting expectations of 2020, which is a rotten combination, especially for mothers," *New York Times* columnist Jen Senior wrote in May. Instead, the stress parents—and especially mothers—experience from mounting economic and time pressures is framed as their individual problem to solve. "Life hacks" for greater efficiency; "self-care" in the form of consumption—the solution to capitalism run amok, we are told, is more capitalism.

IT IS POSSIBLE that the COVID-19 crisis could cause greater numbers of Americans to reject the family norms that have allowed neoliberalism to endure as what Felicia Wong of the Roosevelt Institute calls a "zombie ideology," one whose intellectual claims have overwhelmingly failed to produce. A prolonged and severe recession could cause more Americans to reject the myth that economic security is a byproduct of individual virtue and "good" family decisions. And it could well cause more families—and particularly women—to stop accepting the unrealistic economic and time expectations placed upon them and start demanding public support.

The seeds of such a rebellion were already there. Pre-pandemic, the economic conditions resulting from neoliberal policies—stagnant wages, high inequality—combined with skyrocketing costs of childcare, higher education, and health care had created new political energy for significant new public investments: paid family leave, universal childcare, tuition-free college, Medicare for All, and guaranteed income. None, however, has yet broken through.

Politically, the reason for this is clear: conservatives have blocked any form of public investment for the better half of the last century, and proponents have been unable to build the political will necessary to overcome such entrenched opposition. This is in part due to the resistance of primarily white middle- and upper-middle-class families who have been able to get by, if even on the margins, thanks to the labor of privately paid—and often low-paid—women of color, including many immigrants. Will the current crisis finally prompt a reexamination of those interests? COVID-19 has made domestic labor less available, requiring greater numbers of affluent families to fend for themselves, while forcing domestic workers, who often lack basic labor protections, to make impossible choices between a paycheck and their personal health and safety. The fragility of the moment could help to encourage new thinking, building greater support for solutions that don't require the exploitation of some to ensure the security of others.

Greater demand for public investment could also result from the disruption of public schools, one of the few remaining public benefits for U.S. families. In the wake of the pandemic, vast amounts of additional unpaid labor have been added to already overburdened parents'—particularly mothers'—plates. Studies from May estimate that, since the pandemic hit, working parents have assumed an additional twenty-eight hours of weekly household chores and childcare, with women now performing an average of sixty-five hours a week of household labor (as opposed to men's fifty). Many parents report that they are "failing miserably," as they attempt to juggle work, parenting, and homeschooling.

The crisis has also revealed the risk of relying on private markets to provide essential family goods and services. Public schools are vulnerable to budget cuts in a post-pandemic economy, as states and localities will struggle to balance dramatically reduced budgets. But they will eventually reopen and remain intact. Meanwhile, the privatized U.S. childcare market is crumbling. Most providers operate on razor-thin profit margins, and, amidst widespread closures, are struggling to cover rent and pay staff. The childcare shortages and cost hikes that will likely greet families as local economies begin to reopen (in order to compensate for lower teacher–student ratios that will be necessary to comply with social distancing regulations) could have spiraling negative economic effects, reducing mothers' employment and career-advancement prospects for years to come. And amidst a prolonged recession or depression, the already crippling higher education debt load millions of young people and their families have been forced to incur may become a permanent barrier to the middle class. A public system that bears no responsibility for family health and security is, quite simply, untenable, especially at moments of great peril.

THE OPEN QUESTION is whether the pandemic will serve not merely as a personal tipping point but also as a political one that builds the political will for an alternative economic approach. Such realignment is possible, but barriers remain.

First, it is difficult to overstate the degree to which neoliberals have succeeded in convincing the public—particularly political, policy, and media elites—that their particular form of family values are just a matter of common sense. This has been especially true in the social commentary around family structure, where the talking point that "children do best with two married parents" remains relatively unquestioned, despite the fact that the most rigorous reviews of existing research have found the "literature lacks a clear consensus on the existence of a causal effect" and that "any such effect is small." It is impossible to identify with certainty why the idea remains so persuasive, though like much of neoliberal economics, conservative foundations with a vested interest in the promotion and maintenance of the ideology have invested heavily in efforts to popularize it. And for many elites, who are themselves more likely to have families resembling the ideological ideal, the claim likely has a certain self-serving appeal.

Second, there is no organic political counterforce comparable to what white, evangelical Christian churches provided to neoliberalism. There is excellent progressive organizing across the country, though progressive funders have tended to engage with it—and resource it—through the lenses of political constituencies to be mobilized and siloed policy issues to be advanced. In reality, what is needed is a set of political institutions, united by a set of values and a moral understanding of the economy as a means of promoting human thriving, not growth. Promising models exist in the form of organizing with domestic workers, mothers, and other progressive faith-based communities that are centering caregiving and caregivers, especially the most vulnerable, and building multiracial political bases for greater public investment. But we have yet to fully imagine, never mind build, the infrastructure that the moment requires.

But as the contours of an alternative economic paradigm become clearer, we can also begin to envision the view of families it would enable. There is a possible future in which the public interest in families would actually support the care they provide, not extract it in the form of unpaid labor—and in which the dignity and value of families would be affirmed in an expansive range of forms, not privileging one at the expense of others.

The path to getting there is neither simple nor easy. But the urgency is there. One necessary step in the long journey is to recognize that this health and economic crisis is also a family crisis, meaning that it is rooted in a view of the family that is unworkable on its own and prevents us from truly tackling the problems of the pandemic and the problems of our politics.

INTERNATIONAL LABOR SOLIDARITY IN A TIME OF PANDEMIC

Manoj Dias-Abey

AS MANY GOVERNMENTS began to impose physical distancing measures to slow the spread of the virus, the engines of global economic production ground to a standstill. At the end of April, half of humanity was under some form of lockdown. No one knows for certain the long-term impacts, but in April the IMF predicted that global output per head would shrink by 4.2 percent by the end of this year, almost three times that of the amount logged in 2009 during the global financial crisis. In some cases, the once-creaking welfare systems of rich Global North countries responded with remarkable speed, announcing a range of measures to keep businesses afloat, protect employment, and provide income support to those who have lost their jobs—although Alexandria Ocasio-Cortez has pointed out that the U.S. version, true to form, benefited corporations more than individuals. As Pankaj Mishra put it, "it has taken a disaster for the state to assume its original responsibility to protect citizens." However, citizenship is the fulcrum upon which this newfound social solidarity turns. Workers in the Global South who have lost their jobs as a result of COVID-19 have been left destitute and homeless with almost no support forthcoming from their governments or the international community. Similarly, many migrant workers in the United States fall outside the purview of state welfare aid.

The public health and economic crises caused by the COVID-19 pandemic could provide a clarifying moment: labor keeps the global economy powered, if that was ever in doubt. While the professional managerial class sees out the lockdown in the comfort of their own homes, learning new hobbies and practicing forbearance toward their loved ones, others must continue to go out to work in broadly defined "essential jobs," often wearing no protective gear. We have come to appreciate how broken the labor market has become for the many who work in poorly remunerated jobs under a range of precarious arrangements. But we need to extend this vision to include those to whom we are connected by the economy, planet, and fate.

We must start by recognizing that we live in a deeply interconnected world, and that this is in no small part due to the deliberate decisions taken by Global North countries since the late 1970s. As their leaders lowered barriers to the internationalization of production and finance, firms looking to maintain rates of profit in the face of stiff competition from a newly ascendant Germany and Japan began to offshore production to countries with lower labor costs. In the ensuing decades, complex value chains, crisscrossing the globe, developed to produce goods. Lead firms based in the Global North still control and coordinate the entire production process, while avoiding legal liability for the condition of workers employed by their suppliers. Goods such as food, electronics, apparel, and even surgical masks are now produced in value chains. It is along these modern-day trade and logistics routes that the SARS-CoV-2 virus has spread with such speed and lethality.

The International Labor Organization estimates that over 450 million workers worldwide are employed in value chain–related jobs. Other estimates put the figure at twice as many. Value chains, and by extension those employed in them, have been impacted by two interrelated shocks arising out of the pandemic: first, the lockdown measures aimed at slowing down the spread of the infection, and second, the resulting lack of demand from consumers in the Global North. Already laboring under difficult and insecure conditions, the pandemic has hit workers in these value chains hard. Lead firms have moved swiftly to halt production, in some cases canceling existing orders and refusing to pay for raw materials purchased and production costs incurred. Suppliers in turn have responded by furloughing their workforces without any pay or severance; in the case of Bangladesh, the world's second largest exporter of garments, between 1.2 and 2.28 million have already been affected out of a total of around 4.5 million workers. Although public pressure has forced some companies to pledge unspecified amounts to help workers, as scholar Genevieve LeBaron pointed out on Twitter, the cancellation of orders while collecting government bailouts has once again exposed the hollowness of corporate social responsibility.

Just as our economies depend upon armies of low-wage workers in overseas factories, workers from the Global South also perform vital work inside our borders. Constituting 17.4 percent of the U.S. labor force, migrant workers provide a critical segment in both low-wage industries—such as agriculture, care, and hospitality—and high-wage industries, such as information technology. Some of these workers are naturalized American citizens, others are "resident aliens" or have been brought into the country on a range of guestworker programs (e.g., H-1B, H-2A, and H-2B visas), and yet others are undocumented (for example, it is estimated that 50 to 70 percent of farm workers in the United States do not have authorization to work). Since a significant portion of migrant workers are employed in essential jobs, they must continue to work despite the lockdown, often without the protective gear that would prevent infection. There is no greater evidence of the pathologies at the heart of the U.S. immigration system than the fact that undocumented workers face the threat of deportation on their journey to and from performing this essential work. Although desperately in need of assistance to see this crisis out, farmworkers derived little benefit from the $2 trillion aid package passed by Congress. Resident aliens and temporary migrant workers are similarly excluded from important aspects of the CARES Act.

The pandemic and the near-total shutdown of our economic life will undoubtedly shift our views about the work and lives that we value, and role of the state to provide aid to those whom we see as a part of our community. After decades of neoliberal theory and practice, it is no mean feat to get to once again see the state as a protector of its citizens, rather than a mere facilitator of economic exchange. To seize the moment, prominent labor law scholars have been quick to argue that positive sentiment alone is not enough—we need the institutionalization of a new social contract underpinned by a range of vital employment and labor law reforms. Equally important is a new *global* settlement for work that values and provides for those who stitch our clothes, assemble our electronic goods, pick our fruits and vegetables, and look after our elderly and vulnerable.

What might a new global settlement for work look like? It might be tempting to articulate an ideal theory of international solidarity and then develop a series of prescriptions flowing from that principle. However, we have to start with the world we find ourselves in, not the world of which we might dream. Perry Anderson once suggested that to understand the dominant modes of articulating internationalism, we must first take account of prevailing conceptions of nationalism. A vision of U.S. primacy underpinned by the pathos of white grievance lies at the heart of nationalism today. In the international sphere, this translates as a move toward what some have called a "geoeconomic order," in which the dominant players (the United States, China, the European Union) compete for influence and gain at each other's expense. The pandemic is likely to only hasten this seismic shift in international politics and economics. Trump's announcement that the United States would halt funding to the World Health Organization is only one dramatic step in a slow retreat from international organizations and multilateralism. The embarrassing failure to produce sufficient quantities of ventilators and masks to deal with the health emergency is likely to lead in the medium term to the reconfiguration of value chains—they are likely to become shorter—and the expansion of productive capacity within the state. To some extent, this process was already underway prior to the crisis due to the trade war between the United States and China, but we are likely to see an acceleration. Finally, the trajectory of rising labor unrest in both the Global North and Global South is expected to continue as the imminent economic depression begins to affect profit margins.

This challenging environment presents several opportunities for more international cooperation between labor movements—with bottom-up and top-down dimensions. We should be responding with legal reforms that facilitate this labor movement–driven international solidarity. Some promising cases suggest that shorter and more regionally integrated value chains have more potential for worker organizing. For example, a new farmworkers union in Washington, Familias Unidas por la Justicia, managed to win a labor contract in 2016 by organizing alongside Mexican workers producing for the same distributor. There have also been some tentative efforts by workers employed by suppliers to force lead firms to sign legally binding agreements regulating labor conditions in both domestic suppliers (e.g., Coalition of Immokalee Workers and Migrant Justice) and overseas suppliers (Bangladesh Accord and a gender-justice agreement in Lesotho). Another hopeful development is organizing in the logistics sector, given how central just-in-time production has become to the corporate strategy of lead firms. These efforts have resulted in a better deal for workers employed by suppliers, even if they only represent, at this stage, green shoots. Legal changes to promote these forms of international solidarity must be part of the conversation when we talk about a new labor law settlement. The Clean Slate for Worker Power agenda contains some of the central reforms that would be necessary, such as enabling workers to exercise the right to strike and picket strategically, but we could go further.

In addition, there needs to be a strengthening of the mechanisms of international and transnational labor governance and migration governance. At the international level, the International Labor Organization, which celebrated its centennial in 2019, struggles for relevance in a vastly changed global environment. The International Organization for Migration seems unable to resolve the tension between competing aspects of its mandate—protecting the human rights of migrants and promoting "orderly and regular" migration. While continuing to advocate for the United States to work constructively with and within these organizations, we need to acknowledge that their prospects seem dim in the new geoeconomic order. It might be more fruitful to shift focus to other arenas of transnational governance and treat them as important terrains of struggle. This includes plurilateral trade agreements such as the Comprehensive and Progressive Agreement for Trans-Pacific Partnership (CPTPP), which the Obama administration championed, but Trump abandoned as soon as he assumed office. Scholars generally view some of the innovations for labor governance within the CPTPP positively, although more could be done to shift all aspects of trade (IP, investment, rules of origin) toward a pro-worker agenda. Of course, to repurpose trade agreements for fair trade would require a major rethinking of our current institutions, methods, and objectives. In the migration field, the United States could negotiate bilateral migration agreements with sending states that regulate the labor migration cycle comprehensively rather than relying on unscrupulous labor recruiters. Labor organizations in both sending and receiving states would need to participate in the negotiations. Rich states can play an important role in ensuring that these forms of governance balance the interests of capital and labor more evenly in the global economy, but this will require us to demand that the United States rejects imperialism.

Many of these reforms are unlikely to offer any immediate succor to those living in the Global South. The virus is spreading at an alarming rate in Brazil, India, and South Africa, and the consequences of its inexorable advance are terrifying. We know that the impacts of the virus are likely to be exacerbated in the Global South due to factors such as cramped living conditions and poor sanitation, as well as various existing comorbidities in the population, such as malnutrition, TB, and HIV. Mike Davis reminds us that 60 percent of the 1918 deaths occurred in western India due to factors such as malnutrition. Already burdened public health systems will be overwhelmed. While more than 80 percent of the world's population lives in low- or middle-income countries, they only account for 20 percent of global health spending. Faced with this onslaught and contemplating the loss of remittance income from their migrant workers due to increasing border restrictions, massive capital flight, and onerous debt obligations, Global South countries will have very limited room to maneuver. Global action must consist of a range of measures, including the cancellation of debt, additional IMF lending free from Washington Consensus conditions, and extensive assistance in the field of health, including providing vaccines at an affordable cost to those living in poorer countries. Financial assistance provided to companies based in the United States should be made conditional on responsible behavior toward overseas suppliers.

Pandemics show us that the local can very quickly become the global. In January and February, we watched as those in Wuhan contended with the spread of COVID-19 through their city; we told ourselves that we were safe. However, viruses do not respect national borders, and our interconnected economy means that they can travel along the circuits of capital at lightning speed. The global reach of the pandemic means that we have suffered a set of shared experiences, which allows us to imagine the lives of others in ways that might have been difficult before. This creates radical possibilities for solidarity.

Writing about the meaning that we make out of disaster, Rebecca Solnit observes that "disaster is sometimes a door back into paradise, the paradise at least in which we are who we hope to be, do the work we desire, and are each our sister's and brother's keeper." The pandemic might help us see that it is possible to realize a country where we are responsible for those around us, and this should give us some hope. If we start to see ourselves as each other's keepers, we can demand that our governments also take a more expansive view of their responsibilities in an interdependent world.

A POLITICS OF THE FUTURE

Simon Waxman

EARLY ON THE MORNING of Saturday, May 9, a close friend died of COVID-19. Her name was Fran Morrill Schlitt. She was eighty-four years old.

Fran contracted the virus at her assisted living facility in Boston, across from Symphony Hall. She died nearby at Beth Israel Hospital. I am in Austin, Texas, 1,700 miles away. I was not able to attend the small, brief funeral. I could not be there with her son, David, for the shiva, the seven days of mourning that are traditional in Jewish households. For that week, the community gathers around the bereaved to provide food, conversation, presence.

If I could have joined Fran's community to memorialize her, I would have had a lot to say. Fran and her husband Jacob, who died in 2018, shaped the person I am now. They eased me into adulthood, with all its gravity and mundanity. Fran taught me how to use a dishwasher. She and Jacob taught me about the politics of our city and our nation. They weren't didactic and didn't play the know-it-all.

They encouraged me to recognize that I wasn't alone on the earth and that the others here with me thought differently, had different needs, and were no less entitled to those thoughts and needs. Later I would come to see this way of thinking in terms of public reason: the idea that political choices should be based on principles acceptable to diverse people with infinitely varied ideas about how the world works.

Fran and Jacob were leftists, which, in the contemporary United States, means that the principles on which they reasoned included not just personal freedom but also equality. Equality before the law, equality in treatment by police and public officials, equality of opportunity, and equality in welfare. The policy conclusions recommended by their principles included universal access to mass transit, which confused me because I assumed that everyone, everywhere, rode the subway. They made sure I knew otherwise. Fran introduced me to the idea of single-payer health care when my checkups still came with lollipops.

Although Fran was fifty years my senior, she never gave the impression of believing that she was wiser. She readily asked for help. Sometime in the late 1990s, she called up my mother and asked if I could come to the house to do a little job. It turned out that her computer, always a mysterious object, had become that much more exotic and forbidding. She and Jacob had received an AOL installation CD, and they wanted me to set up email and show them how to use it. They also weren't sure how to use the Web or run their printer. David probably could have shown them, but it was my help they wanted. So for a couple months, I visited regularly, got them online, and helped them stay that way. Although I fooled around with computers, I didn't really know what I was doing. But the idea that two adults might rely on me, a mere bar mitzvah–age kid, was thrilling, and I wanted to make sure I earned their confidence.

At our synagogue I worked with Fran on the kiddush. That's a misnomer; our community didn't have a synagogue. We worshipped in a rented church basement until we moved upstairs to the small chapel, where we draped a white cloth over the cross on the wall. Anyway, every week, after the service, the community gathered for a light snack. The two of us, and usually one or two other kids who had gotten bored of the week's Torah portion, cut up carrots and celery and arranged the chopped vegetables on silvery plastic platters with a container of hummus in the middle. We sliced cheese and filled tiny plastic cups, not much larger than a thimble, with grape juice for the kids and pungent kosher wine for the adults. One small challah was left intact for the prayer over the bread, and Fran showed me how to cut the large one into artfully symmetrical slices. Sometimes there were bagels and other good things. When everyone was finished, she made sure we kids separated the trash from the recyclables. Then we washed the dishes.

Fran and Jacob were not, throughout their lives, motivated to go to synagogue or eat kosher food. From what I came to understand, it was their son's interest that drove them to attend weekly. David and I, and my brother Cobi, all attended the Solomon Schechter Day School in Newton, a Boston suburb. We learned to embody someone's notion of Jewishness, and our parents paid extravagant tuition for an A-plus education in a town that already offered one via the public schools. We came home in the afternoons with Judaically inspired ideas about life and learning, and David imparted these on his parents. This was a feature of being Fran and Jacob. They learned from the young.

Later, after college, after I'd moved back to Boston, I resumed my friendship with them. Both had grown frail, and Jacob a little short-tempered, especially with Fran. They moved slowly and were often sick. In 2014 Jacob—who had spent his life as a labor organizer, civil rights activist, and public servant—won an award from the Democratic Socialists of America. I didn't attend the ceremony, but my brother did. Bernie Sanders had not yet made the DSA hip, but Cobi wasn't the only member of his generation in attendance. Jacob had many friends many decades younger than he. They coalesced around him, and he was galvanized by them.

Jacob's magnetism lay not only in his politics but also his passion for Yiddish. He spoke it and read it and sang in it. Yiddish makes everyone—Fran and Jacob, no less than their young friends—a seedling. To dig up that ancient coiled root would take more days than we are given. Some of the young people who gathered around Jacob were engaged in this same joyful and humbling pursuit. Although Yiddishists spend much of their time looking into the past, their object is always the future—the blossoming, season after season, of the bulbs at the surface end of the root.

The future was Fran's work as much as Jacob's. Fran spent decades practicing and teaching social work. She tried to make better futures for the dispossessed, and she mentored others in that craft. I was never present when Fran was teaching, but I imagine she instructed her students not only in the person-to-person engagement of social work but also in the public good of it. To say that we want to live in a better world is to say that we want to live in a world where people lead better lives—lives that blossom, season after season.

In her later years, Fran took advantage of what she had helped to build. She and Jacob spent days on end at a local senior center, taking part in the activities and the community and receiving support from the social workers there. They attended concerts and received tax abatements, joined memoir-writing workshops and got help arranging in-home care. They would not have needed the validation, but perhaps they were nonetheless gratified. Their lives, spent envisioning and working to realize the future, were now in the hands of the future they had shepherded into being.

I don't know if Fran and Jacob ever thought systematically about their relationships with young people. Did they believe that cultivating the young—the future—was a way to live the politics to which they committed so much of themselves? Was it obvious that working toward a world of freedom, equality, and respect meant taking an interest in the young people who would one day live in and maintain that world? I never asked them these questions. I think a lot of us who subscribe to leftist politics don't ask these questions enough. The young are not really part of the theory, which instead focuses on workers and bosses, capital and labor; colonialism, sometimes; and increasingly racism, sexism, and gender inequity. The big-box media talk about the youth vote in their characteristically emptyheaded way, but a more sophisticated talk of the future doesn't course through the left as it should. Whether we speak abstractly or concretely, it is of philosophies, policies, and histories. We might in addition talk more of futures.

To many Americans, the socialist future that Fran and Jacob pursued seems hellish. A cold and brutal landscape of gray, broken only by blank-faced peasants at toil. If their shackles are not too heavy, they will produce something, also gray, maybe brown. The thing isn't their own. It belongs to a state at once defiantly aloof and always in their heads, their space, their books, their wills, poisoning them with smiling lies about the people.

And yet I can think of hardly anyone who more fully defies this dystopic logic than Fran. Fran toiled, but she did not lose sight of her reward. I hesitate to say that she insisted on it, but I know she took it with pleasure.

In the winter of 2019, she and I spent time in a place as gray and cold as a Soviet mining town, although it was laid low by capitalism rather than anything resembling socialism. I speak of Rochester, New York, an easterly outpost of the Rust Belt. My partner and I had moved there for her job. (We have since moved to Austin for her next job.) Fran had family in Rochester and had come to see them, and me. It was hard for her. By then she had survived lung cancer. She could barely hear under the best of circumstances, and, arched over her walker, she moved with plodding deliberation. One night, we went to a restaurant. It took her fifteen minutes to cover the eighty feet of sidewalk from my car to the restaurant. Then we descended a few steps to the basement-level front door, another labor. Rochester hasn't yet seen its urban comeback, but in contrast to its downtown surroundings, the restaurant was peopled and noisy—so much so that we were often overwhelmed and reduced to silence.

Fran loved her meal. She ate half a chicken on her own, plus potatoes, served on a metal cafeteria tray covered in paper fat-slickened to translucence. She drank two beers, ample pours into glass steins. She leaned in to hear us shout above the racket, and she spoke when she could. She told me how she adored me. She squeezed my partner, whom she had just met.

Throughout her life as I knew it, Fran enjoyed food. Especially in her later years, she was voracious and ate diversely. She cooked and gulped Jewish favorites, to say nothing of a transcendent pea soup loaded with thyme. She also ate the fish in mango chutney, steak, a little bit of everything from the dessert tray. Her mouth would relax into a ring of crumbs.

Last fall my parents and I took her out for her eighty-fourth birthday. We drove to her apartment to pick her up, but half an hour later she still wasn't answering her phone or buzzing us up. I followed another resident into her building, went upstairs, and found her door with its colorful mezuzah on the upper right. Many knocks later, she hadn't stirred. I called her cell phone and her landline, left messages on both. We kept waiting, then gave up. We were halfway home when she called to tell us she had fallen asleep. Would we come back and get her? She could have begged off. She was depressed at the time, struggling alone but still devoted to loneliness. Hardly anyone except the home health aide saw her in those days. Something moved Fran to be with us. So we turned around, and I went up to the third floor again to get her.

Her gloom receded that night as we sat in the pleather-lined booth of a chain restaurant that aspired to outdo the Cheesecake

Factory. Fran had the surf and turf and the dessert and some kind of artichoke dish and the breadsticks, too. We talked about David and how he was getting along in his new home on the other side of the country. We talked about my recent move to Texas. She announced that she would sell her apartment and move into the assisted living facility across from Symphony Hall. This was a decision years in the making, a decision she had resisted, for she demanded independence. When she made her choice, our fears were greatly eased.

A few months later, her refuge proved to be the incubator of the disease that ended her life. But my mother did get chances to visit her there. They had lunch in the dining room. I have a photo of Fran, working intently on a bowl of chicken soup. How I wish I could have sat with her there, surrounded by Ediths and Irvings, Esthers and Evelyns, old and placid with canes and soft hair.

Were we not beset by a pandemic, I would have seen Fran in late April. I feel confident that she would have lived a while longer—maybe six months, maybe a year. Maybe even two. After many health problems, she was doing better. She was evidence that form follows function: by living more happily, beyond the hermitage of her apartment, she had willed herself toward physical recuperation. Surrounded by others, under care and ministration, she had a little more time to look forward to, in which to receive visits from her friends near and far, from her son and his wife, and from the baby they'll soon have.

There was a brief future remaining for Fran, but I don't doubt that she wanted every minute of it. The future was what she had always wanted, which must be why she loved fiercely its citizens: the young. No, like I said, I never asked her this. I just believe it. I believed we would cross Massachusetts Avenue together, I would help her up the marble steps on the other side, and we would go to the symphony.

Fran had a very distinctive voice. I have kept a phone message she left me a few years ago, after her eightieth birthday. She didn't have any big news for me. She insisted that I make rugelach for her eighty-first. She said, "I just wanted you to know that I think you're terrific."

There is a widespread myth, a powerful myth, that the deaths of the aged are never untimely. It is the young who die tragically—their potential unfulfilled and with so many still counting on them. This is true, as far as it goes. Were my brother to suffer some dreadful accident, or fall to a virus, the depth of my pain would be not matched but exceeded by that of his wife and his young children, given all the immediacy and materiality of his gift to their lives. They would have more pieces to pick up than I.

Yet, while no one relied on old Fran like my brother's family relies on him, her death registers as a great loss that arrived much sooner than it should have. Because she was old, every remaining opportunity to be with her was a thing of inordinate value. Our one or two or five occasions to gather again would have been the most central to our friendship. They would have been loadbearing timbers in the temple of memory. Meaning comes to us when we are near the end of something important. Think of your favorite story. The end itself is nothing, a period followed by blank pages. The feeling of the approaching end is everything.

My partner's eighty-eight-year-old grandfather recently died in his sleep. He was one of her closest friends. I don't mean only that their lives were precious to each other. I mean they had more than a past together. They also had a future together, a future whose anticipation made the present gleam. When Grandpa Ralph was struck by a heart attack, their future ended and with it the vitalizing anticipation of more to come. Nothing attainable in life can adequately substitute for that.

About the same time that Ralph passed, about the same time as the virus was finding its way into Fran's home, the lieutenant governor of Texas, Dan Patrick, asserted to a Fox News host that old people would be happy to die from COVID-19 so that the economy might be restored to health on behalf of their grandchildren. Setting aside the fact that the health of the economy is not self-evidently good for children—while the stock market was smashing records last year, almost one in four Texas children was living in poverty—what vision of the future is this? I'm sure it is not a carefully considered one. Patrick is not a careful person. He is a former talk-radio host playing unconvincingly the part of a public servant. He is moved not by a judicious engagement with the problem of the public good but by an instinct for publicity, seeking out the TV camera as a lizard might a sun-heated stone. The lizard needs that heat to live, and some politicians need those cameras to feel righteous and loved.

But even if Patrick doesn't believe what he said, it was thinkable to him, and that tells us something. Though I'm sure he would not say it again today, and though I am confident that even in Texas senicide would never be implemented as policy, I am equally confident that

Patrick and the rest of the state leadership do not care about Fran and people like her, and not just because she lived elsewhere. I live here, and I'm sure they don't care about me, either. I'm a Jew from Boston, probably a liberal, certainly suspect. A foreigner and a virus in the body politic. Patrick would also at least joke about sacrificing me for the good of the young.

That is a claim on behalf of the future. Maybe it is a perverse one, and unserious. But the underlying gesture is real. There is some world apart from our own in which radio blabbers want to live.

I would submit nonetheless that this politics, unlike Fran's and Jacob's, is not a politics of the future. It is a politics of the self. The opposite of the politics of the future is not the politics of the past, although it can seem that way, with the word *Again* so prominent on red hats and in red mouths. But to call this the politics of the past would be unduly charitable. The U.S. right wing calls itself conservative, but it doesn't know the past. It presses the false historical claim that the United States was created to give people freedom from any sort of state-imposed constraint, an idea starkly at odds with the many competing visions of the founding generation. In the Constitution and Declaration of Independence, freedom meant self-rule: law created through fair democratic procedure was legitimate and no offense to liberty, though it might constrain the individual in countless significant ways. It was later that counterrevolutionaries who feared democracy demanded a bill of rights to protect the people from the laws the people wrote. We need not pay even the least intellectual fealty to founding ideals, but we might at least know what they were if we are going to call them our own. Today's right wing is doing something new, as we all must. Something that responds to the world as it is now, not as it was then.

No, the opposite of the politics of the future is not the politics of the past. It is the politics of the self. It's the politics that says damn everything, tomorrow included, unless it brings only what I want. I must get what I want, no matter what you want, and nothing more need be said on the matter.

The opposite of the politics of the future is the refusal of public reason. The unwillingness to think about accommodating the wants and needs of others. What is unthinkable to Patrick, and to at least some of the people who vote for officials such as him, is that anyone could reasonably want something different from what they want, and that these others might even be permitted to have what they want—up to and including their own lives. What is thinkable, if not necessarily desirable, is that people like Fran should piously go off and die so that Patrick and Governor Greg Abbott and the Texas legislature can kick people off the unemployment rolls.

A know-nothing might accuse me of politicizing the death of my friend. But Fran and Jacob knew that everything in life is political. We cannot help, with each passing minute, building the future.

That is not to say that Fran and Jacob spent every waking hour in agitation. This is a caricature of leftists that the contemporary right, with its "funny" memes and its lighten-up strand of anti-PC rhetoric, celebrates. Like most people who share their politics, Fran and Jacob had plenty of festive moments. They joined in a community of worship and kinship. Jacob was a jazz aficionado. Fran had a flair for interesting-yet-unassuming art and fashion. People who constantly protest, who are unable to find pleasure in anything because they understand that everything is compromised by capitalism, are a bore and a chore. I have known some, and though I share their critical perspective, I avoid them.

I take pleasure. I took pleasure in my meals with Fran, even though I knew that the food we ate was provided to us by immigrant farm and restaurant workers demeaned and rejected by the very politics that ensures they labor for the benefit of better-off Americans. The illegal immigrant is enslaved. Denied rights so that her effort is easier to exploit, working for nothing of her own because bosses demand it. Still I took pleasure in those meals.

As Fran reminded us at Jacob's funeral, he desired for all the people, including the despised but essential immigrant, to have not just bread but also roses. The future Fran and Jacob worked toward is anything but gray drudgery. It is full of hard work. But it is also full of rewards. Fran believed that work should pay, which is why she was willing to walk the eighty agonizing feet on a cold night in a city that became an externality, an unwilling sacrifice in the creative destruction of Kodak and Xerox, its bones picked over by Paychex and Wegmans and the United States itself.

Rochester, like the politicians who run Texas and the United States itself, expresses the unremarkable truth that capitalists don't care about people. Fran cared about people. She wanted the chicken and beer in that restaurant because she cared about people.

Does that not make sense to you? Do you not see that everyone's genuine effort—whether traversing eighty feet or a vast south-of-the-border desert—should bring rewards? Do you not see that a moral life entails wanting those rewards not only for yourself but for everyone, for every life is a matter of effort?

Fran wanted pleasure for herself because bread and roses for everyone meant bread and roses for her, too. Her pleasure was the pleasure everyone deserves just for being, because being is hard. She did not believe that people should live austere, gray lives under the thumb of a state that wanted her only to labor and die or maybe just die. She cared about people because she cared about herself. She knew there was enough to go around, and that everyone deserves to have it.

Admit that there is enough for everyone. More than enough. We can have all the bread and roses to satisfy, and so can everyone else, forever, as long as we don't take from others more than we need for ourselves. As long as we don't ask others to toil so that we may hoard the rewards they created—or to die so that the state doesn't have to raise taxes—we can all have chicken and beer. We can all have a livable and beautiful city. We can all have jazz and the future.

GETTING TO FREEDOM CITY

WE SHOULD BE AFRAID, BUT NOT OF PROTESTERS

Melvin L. Rogers

ON MAY 25, George Floyd, a Black man in Minneapolis, was murdered by those sworn to protect and serve. As Floyd pleaded for his life, a police officer pressed his knee on Floyd's neck until his body lay lifeless. We know the image; we have heard the pleas for help, the appeals to show mercy. His death mirrors the recent killings of so many unarmed Black people. As in other instances, Floyd's cries fell on deaf ears—the ears of the officer suffocating him and the three other officers who stood witness to the murder. His death is the latest in an extended history of lynching.

A city burned as rage and anger matched the gravity of Floyd's death. Soon after, a CNN reporter was dragged off live television by police as he reported on the events, and in May the president threatened on Twitter to send in the military to kill protesters—and now has sent federal agents to Portland, where they have disappeared peaceful protesters into unmarked vans. This is where we are: a nation exhausted, slouching (perhaps) toward collapse.

The anger and rage on display in Minneapolis was not only about *police* violence, however. It took place against a broad horizon of state violence, which among other things takes the form of utter disregard for the pain of Black Americans. Amid the revelation that COVID-19 is disproportionately affecting the Black community, we have watched as states reopen their economies and, so doing, ask that same community to sacrifice even more. Little government attention has been given to the structural inequalities of our health care system and the ways it worsens the pandemic's impact on Black life. The toll of COVID-19 in Black America is not merely the result of a lack of access to good health care, it is also due to the way racial bias structures physician engagement with Black people. Whether explicit or implicit, the failure to critically engage this problem, with care and concern, is of a piece with the nation's habit of regularly reminding Black people that their lives don't matter.

This, of course, is further intensified by the recent memory of armed white protesters defying stay-at-home orders. As they flouted public health best practices, white protesters terrorized communities, forced at least one capitol to close, and threatened public officials. These uncaring armed assertions of personal sovereignty were met with little criticism and, in fact, found support from the president. For example, in response to the protests in Michigan, he tweeted: "These are very good people, but they are angry. They want their lives back again, safely!"

In contrast, responding to Minneapolis protesters, and using the words of segregationist George Wallace, he wrote this of the military response he would order: "when the looting starts, the shooting starts."

The invocation of looting always functions as a justification for intensifying harm against Black people and obscuring the initial events that sparked the uprising. That is to say, by focusing on the violence of protests, we suspend criticism of the terror that white Americans daily visit upon Black people, usually in response to some entirely imagined danger: "He didn't respond to the police orders," "I felt threatened by him," and so on. We also blind ourselves to the logic of protests—their quest to rightly disturb the peace in response to injustice—and how much that logic is aimed precisely at producing uncertainty. The uncertainty of protest—both its peaceful manifestation and its chaotic and destructive forms—sits at the heart of its transformative potential.

In recent months, we've faced so many awful revelations: police brutality, the COVID-19 pandemic, the armed claims of individual sovereignty, and a president who plays to the darkest features of human nature and U.S. culture. All reveal the inability of our social and political culture to provide for the common good, and seem to suggest that collapse is close at hand. Indeed, the resources of our political and social culture—what we call democracy—can be exhausted, or at least appear to be exhausted. At that moment, events point to something else on the horizon. The veneer of peace and order disappears. Protesters express a refusal to continue the status quo—the ease with which Black life is extinguished—but it is not clear what is to come. The protesters don't know, and the president doesn't know (although he pretends to have control).

What opens—what is opening right now in this country—is a profoundly unsettled space. Something might emerge, something better than what we have, something more satisfying, and more caring. We've seen the rays of hope in the solidarity produced by Black Lives Matter and the efficacy of local legislative agitation. But authoritarianism could also fill the void—the president is already singing that song. It is the siren song that has empowered murderous neo-Nazis and militias, whose vision matches the president's determination to make the United States the domain of white manhood.

The danger is that we just don't know if the United States is convulsing because it wishes to be something new and better, or is raging to remain something old and twisted. We all should be worried and afraid, but not of the protesters. We should be concerned and fearful that the country may not have the courage to imagine differently, that it may not be able to separate the meaning of freedom from the taking of Black lives. How fitting: the taking of Black life built the country, and that very same logic may bring the country to its knees.

THE PROBLEM ISN'T JUST POLICE, IT'S POLITICS

Alex S. Vitale interviewed by Scott Casleton

ON MAY 25 IN MINNEAPOLIS, George Floyd lay handcuffed and face down for almost nine minutes while police officer Derek Chauvin kneeled on the back of his neck and head. Floyd repeatedly said that he could not breathe. But Chauvin did not relent, and Floyd died of asphyxiation.

Floyd's murder, captured clearly on video, has led to months of protest both at home and abroad. The size and intensity of these protests reflect the pervasiveness of injustice for people of color in the United States. Now more than ever, the role of policing in perpetuating this injustice is being acknowledged and subjected to public scrutiny. There have increasingly been calls to abolish or defund the police.

Such radical rhetoric has made moderate liberals uneasy. They would prefer instead a healthy dose of reform. Alex Vitale, a sociologist at Brooklyn College, is one of the foremost critics of this reformist approach. In his book *The End of Policing* (2017), he comprehensively details the failure of liberal reform efforts to rein in policing—

reforms invariably aimed at producing "better" policing. What this program ignores, Vitale contends, is that the very institution of policing is only a symptom of a larger problem. We must stop funding violent and ineffective policing, Vitale argues, and instead direct that money toward providing social services that underresourced communities need.

In this interview we discuss how we got here, exactly what the problem is, and what can be done about it.

—Scott Casleton

SCOTT CASLETON: Two central themes of your book are the expansion of policing, in terms of increased responsibilities and funding, and the origin and function of policing. Let's start with the first. What has driven this expansion?

ALEX VITALE: To understand police funding, you have to look at the larger structure of economic life in the United States. Over the last forty to fifty years, we've seen a political transformation in the United States. Both political parties have embraced a kind of neoliberal austerity. Under the pressures of global competition, politicians at all levels have decided that the only thing they can do is subsidize the already most successful parts of the economy, in hopes that this will produce a trickle-down effect. And it's driven in part by the fear that no one wants to be Detroit, that cities are under pressure and that there is a need to find some kind of path forward. And the path they've chosen is to embrace high finance, downtown real estate deals, the subsidization of corporate headquarters, and so on.

All this has left cities broke. It has created tremendous wealth for the people who were party to those deals, and then maybe somebody who runs a coffee shop or a food cart gets a little bit out of that, but it has not trickled down into the neighborhoods. This is true across the country. The result has given rise to mass homelessness, mass untreated mental illness, and massive involvement in black markets around drugs, sex work, and stolen goods as survival strategies for the growing number of people who are completely disconnected from meaningful participation in the global economy.

As those people who are left out turn to these other activities, mayors have used the police to criminalize them—to define their behavior as criminal, as an example of individual or group moral failure—and have said that the only way we can manage this is to use people with guns, and to put people in cages. And this is not just a political failure: it's an ethical failure of the highest order, and it has led to the expansion of policing into schools, into the management of homeless people, into the handling of mental health calls, into the demonization of our young people.

SC: You've noted that this trend applies just as well to mayors of ostensibly progressive cities. Do they really think policing is going to help fix the underlying problems of crime and poverty, or do they feel powerless to solve the underlying economic problems, so the best they can do is limit the crime they produce?

AV: I think that the key to understanding this distinction you raise is to acknowledge that we have a deeply flawed political system that has been captured by big money. It assumes that these Democratic mayors are operating on entirely good faith with the interests of the overall citizenry that they represent. But in fact, the largest contributors to local political campaigns across the country are real estate interests, who do not have the interests of the general public in mind, who want to make their downtown real estate deals, and they use all the leverage they can to manipulate this political process, to capture as much of that local, state, and federal money as they can, and to punish politicians who stand in the way of that.

That makes this a story about a set of political choices in a very particular environment—not just of global economic competition, but of big-money politics. What's needed is a radical rejection of that big-money politics and that neoliberal strategy, and it is possible. We cannot accept "there is no alternative." This is a false analysis of the problem, and one of the hopeful things that we're seeing right now is the rise of Democratic Socialists of America, and a whole generation of progressive urban politicians who are trying to push back against this idea. And I think that's part of what's happening in Minneapolis, where they're demanding a total rethink on turning every problem under the sun over to the police to manage.

SC: So, to use the popular slogan, "defund the police" isn't something we do in isolation—it's part of a larger effort to address underlying political and economic problems. Is that right?

AV: So, a few things. One is that the Defund the Police movement understands very clearly what it's about. It was a slogan that could be put on a cardboard sign in a crisis to signal that the solution to our problems is not body cameras and implicit bias training anymore—that we're not going to accept these superficial procedural reforms, that we want to get to the heart of the matter, which is the radical expansion of police power.

Given that, I often say that my book *The End of Policing* isn't really a book about police accountability, it's a book about political accountability. Because the decision to turn social problems over to the police is a political decision (as is the creation of the social problems in the first place). Responding to this deeply entrenched form of governance requires a new politics. We cannot fix policing with a set of superficial, technocratic reforms, because those don't address how the most basic needs of people have themselves been defunded, creating the "crime" that must be policed in the first place. And that dynamic requires a profound political transformation that neither political party's leadership is prepared to embrace right now.

In the short term, there's so much waste, there's so much misspent money in policing that we can start there—defunding and shrinking police forces—and shift huge amounts of resources into communities. But to really fix the problems of mass homelessness, economic precarity, health care disparities, that's going to require more resources—whether that comes from states, or the federal government, or a complete rethink about how taxes are structured in these big cities.

SC: That takes us to the second theme of your book: the origin and function of policing. You often describe policing as a method of social control. This makes it sound like there is someone behind the scenes pulling the strings.

AV: There is someone pulling the strings. It's the politicians who created the War on Drugs, who refuse to build housing, but create police homeless outreach units instead. The police are thus a tool of the state—they are violence workers acting on behalf of the state—but they've been wrapped up in this myth that they're neutral, independent crime fighters, that they're an extension of the law, and that their enforcement of that law is automatically beneficial to everyone. But this view radically misunderstands the actual nature of these legal systems. They do not inherently benefit everyone equally.

There's a saying by Anatole France that "the law in its majesty forbids both the rich and the poor from sleeping under bridges, stealing bread, and begging in the streets." But, of course, the rich don't need to do these things, and by the same token when we create an intentionally racialized War on Drugs, we invariably reproduce racial inequality in the United States. And class inequality as well, because the problematic drug behavior of wealthy people, which is widespread, gets dealt with through clinics, rehab programs, and family dynamics. In poor and non-white communities, these problems get dealt with instead by the criminal justice system, and that makes their lives worse, not better. These interventions are completely ineffective. So we don't need narcotics units to get anti-bias training to fix the racial disparities in the War on Drugs; we need to get rid of the entire legal framework of the war. It is inherently, substantively unjust, and no amount of procedural reforms to policing will do anything to overcome that injustice.

The point is that we cannot only look downstream at very particular policing practices. We also have to interrogate the legal frameworks that are being put in place that then police are being told to enforce. Those legal frameworks serve the interests of some people more than others. They are the glue that holds the whole system together, the root of the problem. This or that incremental police reform will do nothing to dismantle the fundamental logic of the system.

For another example, take police militarization—the focus of a lot of discussion of reform. Militarization is in fact just the most extreme tip of the largest pervasive problem, of turning social problems and political problems over to the police to manage. And as that process has become intensified and we've created more wars against the poor, then we give police more military technology and unleash them on the population. And this is not just about the technology, the equipment—it's also about the culture and the framework, the ethos of policing that comes to see the public as an enemy to be suppressed. But even if we got rid of all of that, a totally lawful, procedurally proper, unbiased drug arrest is still going to ruin some young person's life for no good reason. We can't just get rid of the tanks. We have to get rid of our overreliance on police.

SC: So let's say you get your way and we end the War on Drugs and achieve other kinds of decriminalization, like for "quality of life" crimes and sex work. But not everything can be decriminalized. I take it there will be some remaining residue of criminal behavior—whose job is it to handle that?

AV: We don't know what that residue is going to look like. We really have no idea, because we have concrete, evidence-based strategies to deal with youth violence, homicides, domestic violence, school shootings. This is not about just getting the police out of the homelessness and mental health business: this is about a radical rethink about how safety is produced. When you go into wealthy neighborhoods, safety is not produced by having a police officer on every street corner. Those communities are safe and secure because the people who live in them have safe and secure lives. They have stable employment, and stable housing, and good schools. Well, why can't we have that for everyone?

Once we begin to think this way, all these taken-for-granted ideas about what crime is and how we control it begin to dissolve. And then we see what's left. Yes, people will do bad things, but the idea that the only way to deal with that is people with guns and the use of cages is not necessarily true. Yes, we need systems of accountability and systems of social control, but armed police is not the only—much less the best—way to achieve that.

SC: This goes to a central idea that many people take for granted: police prevent crime. You say this is a myth. Why?

AV: There was a long literature in policing that looked at a whole raft of studies that attempted to perform experiments on this question—to change patrol strength, to shift people to foot patrols, to measure the different densities of policing—and all that research showed no effect for decades. (As police scholar David Bayley put it in his 1994 book *Police for the Future*: "The police do not prevent crime. This is one of the best kept secrets of modern life. Experts know it, the police know it, but the public does not know it.") More recently, there were a few studies, just a few, that were able to show some statistically significant measurable effect for changes in policing. But those effects, while statistically significant, are actually quite small. And what these studies never do is measure the collateral consequences of using policing *as opposed to other strategies*. They never explore the opportunity cost of putting money into policing as opposed to community-based interventions; they never calculate the negative consequences of driving more people into the criminal justice system; they never calculate the financial cost of police, and prisons, and court systems. This work thus happens not just in a data vacuum, but also in an ethical vacuum: it never bothers to consider the consequences, in people's actual lives, of relying on strategies of criminalization.

So even if we can find some small measurable, positive effect for flooding a community with police, that doesn't make it just, that doesn't make it the best solution, and that doesn't mean that the answer is to put police on every corner. The idea that more police and fewer arrests will lead to crime reduction is a gross misunderstanding of how policing actually operates. Preemptive policing takes forms, such as the broken windows theory, that rely on expanding the number of arrests, and even when we don't expand the number of arrests, we expand the number of confrontational and punitive interactions between police and the public—at the same time exposing people to our deeply flawed criminal justice system as a whole, not just to interactions with cops. That's how police enforce their idea of order in an effort to produce lower crime rates. There's no evidence that *this* works. It is deeply harmful to the people who experience it, it produces worse health outcomes, it gives people negative credentials that drive them out of labor markets, and it is just another apology for a rancid politics of divesting from communities and turning it over to the most authoritarian institutions in our society.

SC: Besides the normal political obstacles to reform, what is standing in the way of changing this paradigm of policing? Are police unions a problem?

AV: Police unions are problematic on a number of levels. Let me say that I'm a unionist—a fourth-generation unionist—and I'm not interested in breaking unions. What I'm interested in doing is neutralizing the political power of police unions. To do this, first we have to understand that police unions don't just represent the interests of their members; they've become an institutional focal point for right-wing, neoconservative politics more broadly—especially in big cities, where they may be the only home that people can find for these ideas. And these union leaders are not just playing to their members, they're playing to a larger public, trying to rally these right-wing ideas, and part of what we've seen on the streets recently has really been a *police* counterprotest. The police violence, the attacking of journalists, and so on: they're part of a right-wing movement.

So what do we do about it? I think we have to make their political activities, outside of the collective bargaining process, politically toxic. We have to establish, clearly, that any politician who takes their money cannot be our friend. Anyone who accepts their endorsement does not have our best interests at heart. Not just because it leads to the squandering of money, not just because it leads to contracts that give police a pass on accountability, but because it empowers the most authoritarian, right-wing, and racist worldview that says that the only way that "those people" can be managed is with the threat of guns and incarceration, and that undermines any possibility of a more progressive politics.

SC: Why haven't reform efforts addressed this in the past? Why do politicians push for procedural reforms if there is no evidence to show that it fixes the underlying problems?

AV: Politicians, these big city mayors, have embraced and accepted that they're going to solve their political problems through police, in ways that allow them to avoid any challenges to local economic elites who are driving these neoliberal transformations. When there is a challenge to the abusiveness of policing, the response can't interfere with those economic arrangements that are at the center of their power. So instead they generate a whole series of symbolic interventions that, by design, are incapable of addressing the problem substantively.

Instead of substantive change, they try to give people some comfort that policing will get better, in hopes that their movements will demobilize and that these neoliberal coalitions can get back to the work of downtown real estate development. So they dream up things like implicit bias training that is ludicrous on the face of it: the idea assumes that the root cause of racist policing is unconscious racial bias by individual officers, which completely ignores the way there's *explicit* racial bias in U.S. policing, and also the fact that the racial disparities in policing are primarily rooted in the decision of exactly these mayors to criminalize the behavior of those communities that have been left out of the economic future of their cities.

SC: This places a big emphasis on reform at the level of individual cities. Let me end by asking whether this is where we should focus. How much can be done at the federal level?

AV: The focus right now is primarily on local politics because policing falls under the control of mayors in the United States. But there is a federal issue here. Because the federal government has consistently encouraged these processes, both the economic processes of neoliberal austerity and the turning of problems over to the criminal justice system: Richard Nixon's War on Drugs (expanded under Ronald Reagan), Bill Clinton's 1994 crime bill, Barack Obama's embrace of superficial procedural reforms while continuing to fund police and transfer military equipment.

At the federal level, then, there are a lot of things we should do. We need to totally eliminate the War on Drugs: there should be absolutely no federal involvement in the issue of drugs. We should disband the Drug Enforcement Administration. We should repeal laws such as FOSTA-SESTA that create a federal mechanism for criminalizing sex work. We should get rid of programs such as Operation Relentless Pursuit that flood cities with more federal and domestic law enforcement to further demonize young people. We need to quit incentivizing the hiring of police and the building of prisons, and instead invest in communities. Bring back block grants, bring back support for public housing, Section 8 vouchers. These are the kinds of things the federal government can do to contribute to producing safer communities.

GETTING TO FREEDOM CITY

Robin D.G. Kelley

IN THE SUMMER OF 1969, my mother decided we were moving to Los Angeles. Her friend Luther, an older Black gentleman and fellow devotee of the church established by Paramahansa Yogananda, the Self-Realization Fellowship (SRF), had moved there the year before and sent her letters extolling the city's virtues. It didn't take much convincing. My mother regaled us with Luther's stories, adorning the walls of our tiny New York tenement apartment on 157th and Amsterdam with clippings from *Sunset Magazine* and *Better Homes and Gardens*—images of palm-lined streets, beaches, the Hollywood Hills, gorgeous rooms flooded with sunlight. She imagined herself meditating at SRF's beautiful Lake Shrine property in Pacific Palisades just blocks from the ocean. "The flowers and the weather," she told me recently, "reminded me of growing up in Jamaica." LA would fulfill her dream of having a house, good schools for her children, freedom from violence, and spiritual peace.

But in 1969, all that was only a dream. A single mother with three kids, she survived on low-wage jobs and occasional public assistance. It would take two years for her to board a plane bound for LAX with nothing but a suitcase and a couple hundred dollars. She made the journey alone that summer of 1971, while my siblings and I were with my father in Seattle.

My mother spent her first weeks in Hollywood with Luther before moving into an empty apartment above her aunt's on Ninety-Fourth and South Figueroa Streets. South LA did not at all resemble the pictures that had fed her dreams. Instead of rolling hills and pretty rooms, she found a vast concrete landscape framed on the east by the Harbor Freeway and crowded throughout with dilapidated homes, liquor stores, fast food joints, churches, a smattering of tall palm trees, and Black people everywhere. And cops—lots of cops. She recalls counting fourteen patrol cars lined up on her block one evening.

My mother had fled to LA in search of peace, but instead she found a war zone. Six years after the Watts rebellion, the police patrolled the streets of South LA like a victorious occupying army. But as Mike Davis and Jon Wiener make clear in their monumental new book, *Set the Night on Fire: LA in the Sixties*, the police under Mayor Sam Yorty treated the entire city like it was under siege. "No other major city outside of the Deep South," they write, "was subjected to such a fanatic and all-encompassing campaign to police space and control the night. Along with minorities, many young whites were also routinely victimized, leading hatred of the LAPD to grow into a common culture of resistance." When cops terrorized middle-class white kids for roaming Sunset Strip at night, their cries of "Free the Strip" quickly evolved into "All Power to the People" and "No More Murder of Black People."

The image that lured my mother and millions like her to the City of Angels was painted by racial segregation, patriarchy, sexual norms, classism, and an iron fist used to crush dissent. And yet, the pervasiveness of state violence is not the whole story—it may not even be the main one. *Set the Night on Fire* is, above all, a historical account of how a rainbow of insurgent social movements tried to peel back the glitter, dismantle the police state, and replace elite white rule and its regimes of segregation, militarism, patriarchy, and conformity with a society oriented toward "serving the people."

These social movements imagined a revolutionary culture of care, one that met all basic needs, that eliminated racism, patriarchy, and poverty, and that democratized knowledge and power. Diverse and complex, these movements entangled with one another as allies, affiliates, and adversaries. Some of this history is familiar thanks to an array of brilliant scholars—Rodolfo F. Acuña, Rosie Bermudez, Martha Biondi, Maylei Blackwell, Scot Brown, Ernesto Chávez, Edward Escobar, Dionne Espinoza, Max Felker-Kantor, Mario T. García, Steve Isoardi, Jenna Loyd, Laura Pulido, Bruce Tyler, Daniel Widener, to name just a few. But one of the unique strengths of *Set the Night on Fire* is its focus on "the reciprocal influences and interactions across such a broad spectrum of constituencies," its analysis of movements that are usually treated in isolation. It moves seamlessly between civil rights and Black Power, anti-war protests, gay liberation, women's liberation, alternative media, the Brown Berets and the Chicano Moratorium, student strikes, the free clinic movement, Asian American radicalism, and the citywide struggle against police brutality. All these movements shared a desire for freedom—freedom of movement and mobility; freedom to access public space; freedom to live and work anywhere; freedom to determine their own education, health, and sexuality; freedom to write, perform, and make art; and freedom *from* economic precarity and war—at home and abroad. And at times, Davis and Wiener show, LA's insurgent movements were *winning*, challenging the state's legitimacy and thus driving it to rely on force to maintain control.

Indeed, LA's radical culture was powerful and prevalent. This might explain why my mother never expressed disappointment or regret about moving: the full measure of what she found in South LA in 1971 far exceeded anything she saw in a glossy magazine. She discovered a community of artists, activists, and neighbors who practiced a radical culture that emphasized collective care, survival, community control, and the transformative power of art and politics.

THE SEEDS FOR THIS MOVEMENT had been planted over a decade earlier. South LA residents entered the 1960s with unemployment in the double digits, a median income below the poverty line, and a severe housing shortage. The Black families who could have afforded to leave were imprisoned by restrictive covenants, real estate practices, lending institutions, and white neighborhood associations. In 1963 the Rumford Fair Housing Act attempted to outlaw housing discrimination, but the following year white Angelenos voted overwhelmingly to repeal the law. And the city's response to South LA's economic decline? Add more police.

An increase in police led to an increase in premature deaths. Between 1963 and 1965, police officers killed sixty African Americans—twenty-five of them unarmed, twenty-seven of them shot in the back—and every shooting was ruled justified. But during this period under LA's police state, most Black residents suffered a slower, less spectacular death. Davis and Wiener explain:

> The LAPD operated the nation's most successful negative employment scheme. While giving low priority to white collar crimes, whatever their impact on society, the department fastened a relentless dragnet on poor Black and Chicano neighborhoods. Without the slightest pretense of probable cause, the cops stopped and searched people, particularly young men, in the hope of finding some weed or a stolen item. Those who verbally defended themselves, however innocent, would usually be offered a ride to jail. The result was an extraordinary accumulation of petty arrests (but not necessarily convictions) that made a majority of young men unemployable.

Under such conditions, resistance was inevitable. In 1961, when police arrested a Black teenager in Griffith Park for riding the merry-go-round without a ticket, about 200 African Americans began hurling rocks and bottles at the officers. A year later, when police killed unarmed Ronald Stokes during a raid on the Nation of Islam mosque, over a thousand people rallied against the LAPD and demanded Chief William Parker's resignation. Protests over policing, housing, education, jobs, and racism began to erupt with greater frequency. In the two years before the Watts rebellion of 1965, some 250 demonstrations took place, including a mass march for school desegregation in June 1963. Led by the Congress of Racial Equality (CORE), the NAACP, and the coalition United Civil Rights, it was the largest Black-led march for civil rights in LA history.

The common narrative of the Watts rebellion suggests that the uprising was a spontaneous response to the August 11 public arrest of Marquette Frye (for drunk driving) and the subsequent arrests of his brother Ronald and mother Rena (for intervening). But the history of police repression and Black organizing before the Watts rebellion throws this into question and challenges the prevailing wisdom. Five weeks before the uprising, twenty-two-year-old Beverly Tate was pulled over by two LAPD officers, driven to a deserted street, and raped. The Black press reported the story and the officer, W. D. McCloud, was fired but never criminally charged. Just as protesters during the 1992 LA rebellion demanded justice for Latasha Harlins, the fifteen-year-old fatally shot by storeowner Soon Ja Du in 1991, Black people took to the streets in Watts to demand justice for Tate.

Prior to the Watts rebellion, activists, artists, social workers, and residents had already begun to create a new form of civil society to contend with the growing economic catastrophe. A dynamic urban arts movement birthed the Underground Musicians Association (UGMA), Studio Watts, the Watts Towers Arts Center, Watts Happening Coffee House, the Mafundi Institute, and the Inner City Cultural Center. Some radicalized street gangs formed the Sons of Watts and the Community Alert Patrol (CAP) to monitor police and document misconduct. Others joined the LA chapters of the Black Panther Party (BPP) and US Organization.

Despite sharp differences, these groups shared a desire to end racist policing and envisioned a future based on cooperation, economic strength, and community empowerment. In 1966 the LA Chapter of the Student Non-Violent Coordinating Committee (SNCC) initially proposed that Watts and surrounding communities secede from LA and incorporate as Freedom City. The chosen name harkened back to Reconstruction, when formerly enslaved people established independent towns to secure economic and political power, escape the exploitative hold of the plantation, and develop new forms of justice. This version was no different. When SNCC director Cliff Vaughs first proposed the incorporation plan, he declared, "No resident of Freedom City who has been convicted of a crime and who has paid his debt to society will be denied work because of his past offense." Nor would they be precluded from holding political office or be barred from working in law enforcement. Freedom City gained widespread support from community leaders and Black elected officials but was quashed when the NAACP's national leader Roy Wilkins denounced it as segregationist.

Predictably, the movements committed to reconstructing post-rebellion Watts endured constant surveillance and harassment from the FBI, local police, and agents provocateurs tasked with sowing dissension and destroying property. The state spent more money on repressing a vibrant political culture rooted in art, mutual aid, public safety, care, and democratic practice than it did on creating jobs or affordable housing.

The predominantly Mexican American community of East LA also routinely faced police violence, racism, and divestment. An effort to incorporate in 1960 narrowly failed, leaving LA's largest Latinx community without representation and subject to gerrymandering. Wracked by political and generational divisions, East LA residents initially struggled to mount an effective opposition. Chicano/a youth ultimately broke the political inertia, forming the Brown Berets in 1967 to resist police brutality, and waging a series of "blowouts" (school walkouts) in 1968 to protest segregated schools. These school strikes, involving brown and Black kids, from junior high school to college, comprised some of the largest sustained protests during this period. The fight for better schools—with no police, greater funding, ethnic studies curricula, diverse teaching staff, and freedom of speech and assembly—turned education into the city's central battleground. Campuses became a breeding ground for new multiracial alliances, Third World solidarity, and support for the anti-war movement.

THE POLICE, the FBI, nor Mayor Yorty could imagine folks in South or East LA leading a revolution—so they blamed communists. While their claims were exaggerated, it's true that communists *were* everywhere. Communist Party veterans, Trotskyists, independent Marxists, and associates of the Old Left played critical leadership roles in LA's radical movements. Dorothy Healey, for example, was a longtime communist leader before becoming a pioneering radio talk show host on Pacifica Radio, a labor leader, a peace activist, a key ally in the Black liberation movement, and a thorn in the side of the Communist Party USA's rigid national leadership. And Healey worked closely with California's most famous communist, Angela Davis. Davis had a critical role in LA's insurgent politics and was much more than a renowned political prisoner, icon, and radical philosophy professor. A supporter of the Black Panther Party, an organizer in SNCC, and a formative leader in the Che–Lumumba Club (along with founders Franklin, Kendra Alexander, and Deacon Alexander), Davis was an effective organizer unafraid to push a socialist program even when it ran against the prevailing rhetoric of Black Power. She had earned a reputation as one of California's most popular and beloved revolutionary intellectuals before she was jailed on trumped-up murder charges and her defense rocketed her to international stardom. While Davis delivered withering critiques of state violence, the core of what she wrote and spoke about—in the classroom and in her many political speeches—centered on the meaning of freedom. She understood freedom not as an individual right, as in the liberal tradition, but as a collective, transformative process born from a dynamic struggle for liberation.

One need not count communists to recognize the strong class and anti-imperialist thread running through LA radical political culture. LA's LGBTQ movement first mobilized against police repression, before a radicalized segment sought to create an alternative political culture grounded in anti-racism, anti-imperialism, feminism, and anti-capitalism. Although activist and theorist Carl Wittman was based in the Bay Area, his writings profoundly influenced LA's queer political culture and were foundational to the formation of the Gay Liberation Front in 1970. Wittman's "A Gay Manifesto," published in the *LA Free Press*, argued that genuine sexual liberation required abolishing all extant social institutions that uphold racism, gender and sexual oppression, war, imperialism, class rule, and economic inequality.

Some of the richest examples of LA's revolutionary culture of care come from women's liberation. Feminists built movements centered on health care, reproductive rights, sexual freedom, safety, and the value of reproductive labor. In fact, the welfare rights movement began in LA in 1963, when a Black woman named Johnnie Tillmon founded ANC (Aid to Needy Children) Mothers Anonymous. Tillmon would go on to become the most prominent leader in the National Welfare Rights Movement, founded three years later in 1966. As Tillmon became more involved with the national organization, Catherine Jermany, a Black woman who had been active in various civil rights and Black Power organizations, assumed leadership of the LA County Welfare Rights Organization. According to historian Rosie Bermudez, Jermany established close ties with Alicia Escalante, founder of the East LA Welfare Rights Organization (ELWARO). Although Wiener and Davis tell Tillmon's story, Jermany, Escalante, and ELWARO are significantly absent from *Set the Night on Fire*. Escalante was one of the most effective organizers in East LA, and her work with Jermany speaks to the challenges of building Black–brown solidarity during the late 1960s and to the extraordinary radicalism of welfare rights. Black and Chicana welfare rights activists built a movement for racial, gender, economic, and reproductive justice. They defined childcare as essential labor, demanding women receive an adequate income regardless of whether they worked for wages or stayed home to raise children. Moreover, they insisted on complete reproductive control of their bodies. For Black, Latinx, and Native women, this meant not only having the right to abortion care, but also having protection from forced sterilizations.

At stake was adequate, competent, and affordable women's health care. Even in California, which granted women the right to "choose" in 1970, many women could not afford an abortion—or pre- and postnatal care and regular gynecological visits, for that matter. In 1971 Carol Downer and Lorraine Rothman opened the Feminist Women's Health Center on Crenshaw Boulevard. They were pioneers in the women's self-help movement to demystify medical authority in a profit-driven, sexist health care industry, providing information about birth control and abortions and teaching women skills such as self-conducted cervical exams. They were also a threat to the district attorney and the county medical examiner. In 1972 the LAPD raided the center after learning that women were told to use yogurt to treat yeast infections. The police arrested Downer and Colleen Wilson for practicing medicine without a license, a charge that didn't stick. Not only did the center prevail, but Downer also launched similar centers all around the country and the world.

Before the Feminist Women's Health Center, there was the LA Free Clinic. Founded in 1967, it was the second such clinic in the country (the first was established in San Francisco's Haight-Ashbury district). By 1969 the LA Clinic served some 1,200 people a day, providing medical, mental health, and even legal services. The clinic operated at night, owing to the fact that the staff were primarily volunteers who worked day shifts as doctors, nurses, psychologists, and lawyers. It was an incredible experiment in mutual aid and anti-capitalist care, and not simply because services were free. The staff prided themselves on working without judgment or bureaucracy, free from a criminal justice system that criminalized illicit drug use and addiction—which meant breaking the law when necessary. Clinic doctors performed abortions, ignored drug laws, provided drug counseling, and encouraged the use of psychedelic drugs in some cases. The LA Free Clinic set out to remove medical care from the marketplace and reimagine care as a community project rather than a commodified service. Its commitment to "serve the people" inspired similar free clinics throughout the city. In May 1969 the Brown Berets opened the Barrio Free Clinic in East LA; two months later, the Peace and Freedom Party helped found the Long Beach Free Clinic; and in December 1970 the Black Panthers opened The Alprentice Bunchy Carter Free Clinic, named after one of the Panthers fatally shot on UCLA's campus by Claude Hubert-Gaidi, an FBI operative posing as a Panther. Overall, during the formative years of the free clinic movement, California was home to a third of the nation's clinics, and over 80 percent of these were located in Southern California.

In 1972 the massive benefit concert to commemorate the seventh anniversary of the Watts rebellion, Wattstax, occurred at the LA Coliseum. The concert was intended to celebrate Black culture and identity and to showcase community progress, but in reality it masked a hard truth: working people in South LA had not experienced any appreciable socioeconomic change. Wattstax coincided with my mother's one-year anniversary as an Angeleno. By then the glitter had begun to dull. Jobs were harder to find. She noticed an uptick in burglaries. The arts community had thinned out. And then, in May 1973, the city regained some of its sparkle for my mom and a whole lot of folks in her neighborhood when Tom Bradley defeated Sam Yorty: LA had its first Black mayor.

Bradley had been a police officer since 1940. He entered politics in the 1950s; in 1961 he won a seat on the city council. He nearly defeated Yorty in 1969 by running as a progressive fighting for fair housing, civil rights, jobs, and an end to police brutality. This campaign would have been impossible without the wind of radical social movements at his back. Bradley's 1969 mayoral campaign revealed that a progressive agenda could flourish. But his campaign perished because he underestimated the forces resistant to change.

Bradley did not make the same mistake in 1973. Remaking himself as the classic neoliberal big city mayor, he made peace with developers and finance capital. Bradley's election marked the beginning of the end for LA insurgent politics. With the help of his investors, he preserved the city's glitter and added some more color. South and East LA experienced massive disinvestment at the expense of downtown and Pacific Rim capital, even as Bradley championed the preservation of the Watts Towers and supported museums and public art projects preserving the city's multicultural heritage. "Bradley's greatest accomplishments," write Davis and Wiener, "were not his attacks on residential segregation or direction of public investment to have-not neighborhoods, but rather the rebirth of downtown property values and the creation of a state-of-the-art infrastructure for the globalization of the metropolitan economy in the 1990s." The ex-cop turned mayor could not rein in the police or police chief Daryl Gates.

The LAPD shooting of unarmed Eula Mae Love, the fifteen Black men killed by chokehold, the tightening repression of Black and brown neighborhoods under the guise of the War on Drugs, the killing of Latasha Harlins, the beating of Rodney King and the subsequent rebellion of 1992—all happened under Bradley's watch. Today LA remains segregated, overpoliced, and even more economically unequal than it was in 1961.

I BEGAN READING *Set the Night on Fire* as the world took shelter from the deadly new coronavirus. I had dreams of free health care for all, buildings that once caged people turned into libraries and schools, community centers serving the people homegrown organic food, embracing confinement as a way of reimagining the world outside our windows. By the time I finished the book, millions had broken quarantine to protest the murder of George Floyd and countless others killed by police or vigilantes. Here in LA, multiracial waves of demonstrators converged in the centers of wealth, power, and commerce—Beverly Hills, Santa Monica, the Fairfax District, West Hollywood, Downtown. They called for defunding the police and investing in education, health care, housing, living wage jobs, and—in the words of the People's Budget LA Coalition—"Reimagined Community Safety."

Meanwhile in South LA, artist Lauren Halsey was knee-deep in her own revolutionary project long before the protests or COVID-19. A third-generation Angeleno born and raised in South Central LA, Halsey creates powerful installations celebrating her community's resilience, creativity, and resistance to displacement and erasure, both as a reclamation of history and a projection into the future. Although she was born in 1987, Halsey, more than any other artist, is heir to the community arts tradition of the Watts Renaissance. She is less interested in winning the recognition of the art world than in building a community center. She told one interviewer: "With all of the odds already stacked against working-class Black and brown folks in low-income neighborhoods in LA (food, education, police, housing, etc.), I can't imagine not having a community-based practice. My interest is to not only affirm folks through my practice/the artwork but most importantly to do so with tangible results: paid jobs, transcendent programming, free resources, and workshops." And she walks the talk, hiring Black carpenters at union wages through the LA Black Worker Center—a South Central institution also headed by a radical Black woman, Lola Smallwood-Cuevas. Just as Halsey and her renegade crew—Monique McWilliams and Korina Matayas, among others—were preparing to launch the Summaeverythang Community Center, COVID-19 struck. Halsey pivoted, turning the community center into a food bank. Every week she and her crew box and deliver thousands of pounds of organic, locally sourced produce to the Nickerson Gardens housing projects and other low-income families in Watts. Free. Free of pesticides, free of GMOs, free of obligation, free of stigma, free of charge. Survival pending revolution.

For many self-styled leftists, images of overturned police cars or gun battles between Panthers and SWAT are the glitter that shrouds the radical tradition of care and mutual aid. The Summaeverythang Community Center is the bearer of this radical tradition. So are the LA Black Worker Center, the Strategy and Soul Movement Center (a project of the Labor/Community Strategy Center), the Los Angeles Community Action Network, and the Mutual Aid Network LA, among others. Unless we clean the glitter from our eyes, as my mother did almost fifty years ago, we might not see it. Perhaps Freedom City is on the horizon after all.

TEACHING AFRICAN AMERICAN LITERATURE DURING COVID-19

Farah Jasmine Griffin

I HAVE BEEN TEACHING African American literature to college students for almost three decades. This year my students in Introduction to African American Literature started the semester in a lecture hall on the campus of Columbia University and ended it scattered to the four corners of the Earth. Some had to quarantine for two weeks after returning to their countries. Others remain in rooms and apartments in New York, an epicenter of the pandemic. Some have lost family members; others have themselves been sickened by the virus. Some turned out to be more comfortable talking on Zoom than in a physical classroom; others find it alienating and prefer instead to reach out through email or on WhatsApp. And still they kept reading, they kept thinking. They showed up, week after week. Teaching them in this pandemic shed new light on the power of learning, community, and this extraordinary literature.

I missed my students terribly. Nonetheless the moment allowed us to work together in a different way. The crisis stopped us in our tracks, but it also provided an opportunity. I decided to slow things down for them. Rather than continuing to read a novel a week, we read an essay and a short story by James Baldwin, one of Toni Morrison's shorter novels, and, in the semester's last two weeks, Octavia Butler's *Parable of the Sower* (1993), a work of speculative fiction that portrays community-building in the midst of economic, social, political, and ecological catastrophe. Ultimately Butler's novel—in which change and adaptability are major themes—encourages readers to consider what kind of future might be built on the other side of pandemic and the catastrophe of racial injustice that it laid bare. How fitting.

My course changed in other ways as well. I canceled the take-home exam, which would have required students to provide a synthesis of their learning and to place texts in conversation with each other. Instead, I decided to focus on imaginative skills, and asked the students to create a work of art in response to any of the texts we had read. I also gave them a second assignment, to be shared on the last day of class. The description began with a quotation from Arundhati Roy's essay "The Pandemic as Portal":

> Historically, pandemics have forced humans to break with the past and imagine their world anew. This one is no different. It is a portal, a gateway between one world and the next. We can choose to walk through it, dragging the carcasses of our prejudice and hatred, our avarice, our data banks and dead ideas, our dead rivers and smoky skies behind us. Or we can walk through lightly, with little luggage, ready to imagine another world. And ready to fight for it.

The description of the assignment followed.

As we pass through this portal, let's think about what we might take to the other side, and what we want to leave behind. One or two sentences per question. No more.

1. What one book from class would you want to take with you?
2. What, if anything, from your old life do you want to leave behind?
3. What do you appreciate that you would like to take with you?
4. What change, if any, would you like to see, and commit to bring about, on the other side?

Together the two new assignments—the response to the Roy quotation and the creative project—asked students not only to think about what they had read, but also to make, build, and imagine. Morrison said that in moments of crisis, "Artists go to work. . . . That is how civilizations heal." In addition to their analytical skills, which were on display in every class, I wanted my students to stretch their imaginative ones as well.

My students did not disappoint me. In this season of unimaginable death, especially Black and brown death, these young people rose to the occasion. With careful consideration of the books and for each other, with a strong desire to help heal the world in which we live, they went to work. They created poems, paintings, and book covers inspired by Zora Neale Hurston, Gwendolyn Brooks, and others. One student, Alexzundra, an especially talented writer who was inspired by a scene in Hurston's *Their Eyes Were Watching God* (1937), read an original prose poem over a short, meditative film: "Have I been captured, seen my reflection without seeing my face?" Another, Douglas, submitted a pencil drawing based upon the end of *Parable of the Sower*, imagining a new world rising like a phoenix from the ashes of the old. Butler also sparked the creativity of several musicians. Nigel and James each composed, performed, and recorded original songs inspired by the novel. Nigel's lyrics and acoustic guitar sought "to capture the moral relativism of Lauren's [Butler's protagonist] travel sonically," while James explained that he used "the chord progression to emphasize the importance of the word change. A new chord is cued each time the word is said." He then recorded himself playing jazz trumpet solo over the chord progression. A third musician, Esther, recorded her solo piano medley of songs, from Ray Charles to Frédéric Chopin, that capture the works we've read. Ralph Ellison's *Invisible Man* (1952) inspired Justin and Isaac to write first person narratives that I hope are just the beginning of longer works.

In answering the last of the four questions prompted by Roy, most of the students expressed the desire to leave behind the drive to be busy for the sake of being busy, and to part with performances of self that feel inauthentic to them given the current crisis. Instead, they want to cultivate community. Significantly, they committed to addressing inequality, injustice, and environmental disaster. They want to join and create organizations and institutions committed to bringing about significant social change.

Because I strongly believe in the power of art and creativity, I hoped these assignments would allow my students to slow down and dig deep inside of themselves. They did and emerged as visionaries, just the kind of people we need now: global citizens, gifted with creativity and imagination, and capable of imagining a more just future. I hope to live to see the world my students create. As their teacher, I will do all I can to make sure they are able to do so.

CONTRIBUTORS

Anne L. Alstott is Professor of Taxation at Yale Law School and author of *No Exit: What Parents Owe Their Children and What Society Owes Parents.*

Dan Berger is Associate Professor of Comparative Ethnic Studies at the University of Washington at Bothell and coeditor of *Remaking Radicalism: A Grassroots Documentary Reader of the United States, 1973–2001.*

Scott Casleton is a PhD student at the University of California, Berkeley studying political philosophy and intellectual history.

Manoj Dias-Abey is a socio-legal researcher at the University of Bristol School of Law.

Leandro Ferreira is head of the Brazilian Basic Income Network.

Vafa Ghazavi is a doctoral candidate and John Monash Scholar at Balliol College and Lecturer in Politics at Pembroke College, University of Oxford.

Gregg Gonsalves is Assistant Professor in Epidemiology of Microbial Diseases at Yale School of Public Health and Associate (Adjunct) Professor of Law and Research Scholar in Law at Yale Law School.

Colin Gordon teaches History at the University of Iowa, and is the author of *Citizen Brown: Race, Democracy, and Inequality in the St. Louis Suburbs.*

Farah Jasmine Griffin is Professor of English and Comparative Literature and African American Studies at Columbia University and author of *Harlem Nocturne: Women Artists and Progressive Politics During World War II.*

Paul Hockenos is author of *Berlin Calling: A Story of Anarchy, Music, the Wall and the Birth of the New Berlin.*

Amy Hoffman is author of *The Off Season.* She teaches Creative Writing at Emerson College and the Solstice Low-Residency MFA Program at Pine Manor College.

Walter Johnson teaches History at Harvard University and is author of *The Broken Heart of America: St. Louis and the Violent History of the United States.*

Amy Kapczynski is Professor of Law at Yale Law School and cofounder of the Law and Political Economy blog.

Paul R. Katz coordinates the Jain Family Institute's work in Brazil and is a PhD candidate in Latin American History at Columbia University.

Robin D.G. Kelley, Professor of American History at UCLA, is author of *Africa Speaks, America Answers: Modern Jazz in Revolutionary Times.*

Julie Kohler is Fellow in Residence at the National Women's Law Center and a senior advisor to the Democracy Alliance.

Adele Lebano is a visiting researcher at Uppsala University.

Shaun Ossei-Owusu is Assistant Professor of Law at the University of Pennsylvania.

Jason Q. Purnell is Associate Professor and Director of Health Equity Works in the Brown School at Washington University in St. Louis.

Jamala Rogers is author of *Ferguson is America: Roots of Rebellion.*

Melvin L. Rogers is Associate Professor of Political Science at Brown University and author of *The Undiscovered Dewey: Religion, Morality, and the Ethos of Democracy.*

Sunaura Taylor is author of *Beasts of Burden: Animal and Disability Liberation.*

Alex S. Vitale is Professor of Sociology at Brooklyn College and author of *The End of Policing.*

Simon Waxman has written for the *Washington Post*, the *Baffler*, *Los Angeles Review of Books*, the *Boston Globe*, and *Democracy Journal.*